MW00478131

Life That Will Always Be

Everything You Have Ever Wanted to Know About the After-Life

Life That Will Always Be

Everything You Have Ever Wanted
to Know About the After-Life

DR. ROB COVELL

LIFE THAT WILL ALWAYS BE:
Everything You Have Ever Wanted to Know
About the After-Life
Dr. Rob Covell

© Printed 2021

ISBN - 978-1-7325276-9-0

Quest Theological Institute

A Division of Quiver Full Publishing

Cover and inside design layout
Carolyn Covell

Printed in the USA

Dedication

This book is dedicated to The Refuge Community. This community is an amazing family of truth seekers, God chasers, and radical worshippers who make the journey of spiritual formation a joy! I appreciate your continued partnership and your faithful prayers as I wrote this book. You all are the closest example of what a true apostolic community of Christians looks like in the Modern Era. Some day Church historians will write about the expression of Christianity that will emerge from this very unique community of disciples.

This work is also dedicated to those who seek theological truth and desire an expression of Christianity that is healthy, dynamic, and Spirit-filled in the Modern Era. Deep down truth seekers know that there is more to our faith than religious rituals and forms of religion that lack power.

I also dedicate this book to those who are curious about all things eternal and who are seeking answers, those who mourn for the loss of loved ones, and those who need comfort and resolution by knowing what the Bible says about eternal life.

Acknowledgments

Carolyn Covell - My loving wife and forever covenant partner in this life. I am thankful for the life we share as we pursue Jesus in every season. My books are great because of your hard work, prayers, and love. I also want to thank my family for their constant support and prayer.

The Refuge Community - Thank you for your amazing hunger for God, the pursuit of the supernatural, and demonstration of authenticity as you love God and His people. You are truly a joy to serve and pastor. I am grateful for what we have accomplished in the Lord, with our sights on many more days as we go from glory to glory together.

Dr. David Collins - Thank you for being a great spiritual father, a wise counselor, and an example of what a man of God is like. You are a modern-day apostolic model for us to pattern our lives after.

Dr. Che Ahn - Thank you for leading the HIM Apostolic Network with wisdom, godliness, and vision for the future of the New Apostolic Reformation Movement.

Papa Mark Tubbs - Thank you for your tender care, strong leadership, and encouragement in my life.

Papa Wendell McGowan - Though I am just getting to know you, thank you for speaking into my life and receiving me as a spiritual son.

My Colleagues, Friends, and Staff at The Refuge Community - Pastor Christine Monroe, Prophetess Yvonne Camper,

Pastor David Frondarina, Pastor Kylene Frondarina, Victor Perez, Steven Navarette, Jeremy Wood, and Adrian Brown; thank you for doing life with me as we experience the great things that God does together. I also want to thank The Refuge Community Elders for their amazing leadership abilities, wisdom, and courage to obey God and advance the Kingdom!

The Great Community of Franklin, Tennessee - Your community has been a writing refuge for me and your friendly spirit is an oasis of goodness in our nation. May God bless your city and prosper the people. From the tremendous struggle of losing the Civil War to embracing the Civil Rights Movement, your community's commitment to an equitable future for all people will prosper you.

Contents

Introduction

*L*ife That Will Always Be is an overflow of many conversations and questions from friends at church, hurting families who lost loved ones, and the curiosity that people have about what happens to us in the afterlife. My prayer is that you, dear reader, are resolved, confident and hopeful about your eternal destiny after your sojourn here on this wonderful planet that God designed for us to enjoy. To have the questions about what happens to us when we die answered, helps us live this life in the present age with hope and helps us find comfort when we lose those we love.

The Scriptures teach that this life is but a mist. According to James 4:14, "What is your life? For you are a mist that appears for a little time and then vanishes." The thought of mortality can either frighten or encourage us depending on what we believe to be true about what happens when this life is over. Eternal life is perhaps the most popular theological subject with Christians and non-Christians alike. Supernatural content pervades popular culture in the West because people know there is more to this life. Our cultural superstitions have survived the centuries, and deep down at our core, every person on earth knows that there is more to our existence than meets the eye. I suspect even atheists in the dark night of the soul have contemplated the great unknown of the afterlife and the abyss of death that seems like a terrifying nothingness of silence. If this human experience is all there is to life, then that indeed is a weak and pitiful philosophy and worldview to embrace. Romans 1:18-32 teaches that God has proved His existence and eternity is written on our hearts.

Fortunately, the Scriptures not only answer our questions about the spiritual realm, heaven, the resurrection of the dead, and eternal life, but they also invite us into the mystery of loving and knowing God and experiencing the joy that flows from an amazing authentic relationship between the Creator and the ones created in His image. The Scriptures paint for us a complex tapestry of cosmology and creation in the context of a loving Father God who makes good on His promise to restore to humanity what was lost in the Garden of Eden. Physical death and the disembodied soul are but an intermediate state as we wait for the new creation to come. *Life That Will Always Be* begins the journey of hope that will comfort the soul, break the fear of death, and release you to celebrate the great life we are given by God: A life that was designed specifically for you by the Father of Llights; the life ransomed for you by His obedient Son.

CHAPTER 1

WHAT IS ETERNAL LIFE?

"Then the LORD God formed the man of dust from the ground and breathed into his nostrils the breath of life, and the man became a living creature."
Genesis 2:7

At the very beginning of the Bible, God proclaimed His Creation that He made was "very good." This describes the satisfaction the Godhead experienced, as the Holy Trinity celebrated the Creation from the cosmos to humanity, which includes every form of creation in between these two vast and wonderful expressions of God's power and beauty. The Genesis account opens our minds to the wonder of a perfect world where chaos, death, and disorder are alien invaders that have no place or purpose in the perfection, benevolence, and peace the created order enjoyed before the Fall in Eden. God is life, for all life emanates from Him. In God, there is no death; only life that will always be. Therefore, death is the condition of being absent from a relationship with God.

The Genesis narrative gives us insight into the type of life that God describes as eternal life. The symbolism contained in the Genesis creation account is the starting point for us to begin to understand the subject of eternal life. First, we see that God self-exists. Genesis 1:1 teaches us that "In the beginning, God created the heavens and the earth." This verse invites us into the mystery of contemplating the nature and character of God who is timeless, self-existent, all-powerful, possessing infinite wisdom, awesome, and, most importantly, Fatherly. The action of God creating is a beautiful expression of love that opens the mind to wander and explore the dimensions of grace that God extends to those who are made in His image as we think about the world in which we live. This is a life that emanates from God, is given by God, and is sustained by God. A world designed without death.

No Death in Original Design

As the Genesis narrative unfolds, a picture of God begins to emerge revealing His infinite wisdom in the complexities of the created order as it begins to take shape. The created order including the vast expanses of space, stars, and planet earth paints a picture of a universe designed to host humanity, who are the object of God's love. This description of a created cultivated planet that would become the home of humanity in the Genesis narrative excludes the concept of death. We do not see in the Genesis narrative God designing death as an integral part of His creation. What we do see is that God is the author of life. Life exists because He exists and He wills life to exist by His sovereign desire. The intelligent design of life reaches its crescendo in Genesis 1:26-28 with the creation of humanity, male and female, and the blessings of divine favor and dominion that the Godhead spoke over our representatives, Adam and Eve. The grace of being made **imago Dei**, the crown of God's created work, is expressed in all the multi-dimensional ways that humanity expresses: genius, creativity, invention, and any other way that displays the multifaceted beauty of man being made in God's image and likeness.

God's created order is the revelation of the mind of God in living color. It is experienced in the physical realm in which we live, move and have our being. Not only does humanity rule over God's creation, but we also exert God-given dominion over creation, as we work to expand human influence over the earth God gave us to steward. Genesis 2:15 shows us how God moved as a Father and placed Adam in the center of His perfection on earth - Eden - and mandated Adam to care for it and work to keep it. The Hebrew word for "work," **ābad**, means "to work; serve; or serve another as a laborer." This implies that a type of self-sacrifice and humble service to God caring for the creation He charged us with is an expression of co-laboring with Him. The Hebrew for "keep," **šāmar**, means "to guard; give heed; revere; save a life; observe; and watch." This implies that humanity should co-labor with God to expand Eden and maintain the beautiful inheritance that God has given to humanity. Repeatedly, the creation narrative in Genesis 1 and 2, paints a picture of perfection, calling, destiny, and adventure as humanity expands the perfect creation: the idea of Eden across the earth by multiplying, managing, building according to God's design. The Genesis narrative never mentions death as part of God's original design. The last point in the Genesis narrative which speaks of the untouched perfection that was designed without death is the deep and wonderful verse, Genesis 2:25: "And the man and his wife were naked and were not ashamed." So much theological truth is compressed into this verse. As we unpack it, we learn that the absence of shame is the absence of sin. Where sin is absent, death has no invitation to exist. Where death does not exist, eternal life is preeminent and the prevailing reality. This is the glory of the original design of the human experience by God. The story of Scripture is the unfolding revelation of how God worked through the time-space continuum to re-order and reorient His creation back to His vision of unbroken, eternal life with the objects of His love: humanity.

The Tree That Tests Love

In Genesis 2:16-17, the Lord God gives man a commandment not to eat the fruit of the knowledge of good and evil. This reveals that the only revelation God desired for humanity was the revelation of Himself in the creation that testifies to His awesome power, intellect, and beauty through their relational experience with Him. Humanity was never designed to know evil. The Hebrew word for "evil" is **ra**. It means "bad; evil; malignant; wicked; worse; injurious; wrong; immoral; misery and distress." These are things that are symptomatic of the presence of corruption in creation, inter-relational corruption, and the death that flows as the consequence of eating from this forbidden tree. Pain would become the reminder of the consequence of that choice. God said man would "shall surely die" as the wages of the sin of disobedience. The existence of evil in the created order is not by God's design, but by humanity's allegiance with the agent of death, Satan, and the deception that veils humanity to the influence of personalized evil.

Why would the Lord God place a tree in Eden that could become the poison that would color the world and the human experience with pain and death? The answer is simply for love. God never designed humanity to be physical/spiritual drones. The type of creation that is the essence of the human experience is one being made in the image and likeness of God. Humans are free moral agents with the complexities of possessing all of the graces and expressions of what being made in the image of God involves. 1 John 4:16 declares that "God is love" and in this way, authentic love can only be expressed in the context of a free will relationship where each party is free to love and express affection that is not coerced. The Tree of the Knowledge of Good and Evil is the tree that tests love. The origin of death was the consequence of disobeying love.

Though death came from the Tree of Knowledge of Good and Evil that tested love, life was found on another tree that would become the center of the redemption of humanity. Just as the Tree of Knowledge of Good and Evil was at the center of the garden, the tree of life, the cross of Jesus Christ, is at the center of the world and is the hinge point that all human history revolves around. The cross is the demonstrative evidence that the Father would fulfill His promise to restore humanity to Eden and redeem the human race from the tyranny of death. In Genesis 3:15, God gives humanity hope that a Second Adam, a Messiah, would prevail against the serpent, crushing his head. This symbolic language of defeating the authority of Satan who now rules a dominion of death in Genesis 3 looks across the time-space continuum to an age where it is replaced by the fullest manifestation of the kingdom of God, which is a kingdom of eternal life.

Genesis 3 details the temptation in Eden, the deception of the serpent, God's response to the offense, and the promise of Messiah, laying out the epic saga of redemptive history that is revealed in the prophecy of Scripture, and ultimately in the Man, Jesus Christ. The revelation of Jesus is the revelation of eternal life. He is the physical living reality and the guarantee of eternal life in His resurrection. Jesus said He is "the Life," meaning He is the Second Adam who would obey the Father, fulfill every type and shadow of prophecy in the Word of God, model the fullness of the human existence, and in His death and resurrection, reverse the curse of death by securing eternal life for those who would believe this beautiful gospel of the Kingdom. The tree that tested love, is replaced with a tree that demonstrates love: the cross.

Jesus said in John 14:6, "I am the Way, and the Truth, and the Life. No one comes to the Father except through Me." Jesus is the only way that leads humanity back to the original design of a created order that is un-marred and perfect, a design that excludes death. The journey to the glorious perfection of a restored Eden begins by faith in the sacrifice of Jesus for the sin that lives in each one of us, and the resurrection that speaks of the restoration to come. The Christian faith is God's agency by which He would not only free individuals from the bondage of the Fall, but restore even the created order: the Genesis 1 and 2 reality of perfection, a world freed from the effects and influence of death.

The Definition of Eternal Life: Shadow Life that Reveals Common Grace

Eternal life in its simplest definition is a life that is in relationship with God because He is life, possesses life, and gives life. Consequently, if one does not have a relationship with God, they do not have eternal life. The Scriptures teach us that a person who does not have a relationship with God, does not have life, but death. Jesus said in

Matthew 8:22, "Follow Me, and leave the dead to bury their own dead." Jesus is describing the human existence of a life apart from Himself. Though these people are animated and live a human experience in creation, they are spiritually dead, headed for physical death, and ultimately an eternal death that is called the Second Death in Revelation 2:11; 20:6; 20:14; 21:8. This is the simplest Biblical definition of eternal life.

The human experience in this life apart from God is a shadow and mist of the eternal life that Adam and Eve enjoyed with God before the Fall in Eden. To live this life without God is still certainly a type of grace from God, in that everyone experiences some joy, makes memories, enjoys family, does some type of work, finds some type of identity, and finds some goodness in a corrupted world colored in the shadow of coming death. Theologians call this the common grace that God gives to all people living in His creation. It is also grace from God to make an opportunity for humanity to love Him as He pursues orphaned sons and daughters in the Gospel of Jesus Christ. God is Fatherly and benevolent to give us a shadow life of eternal life that causes each one of us to consider the question, "What happens after this life?" The pursuit of the answer to this question reveals that eternity is written on the human heart and is hard-wired into the soul of every human being.

Every organized culture has a theology of death and eternal life, even atheism is a theology. Its theology and world-view deny the witness of creation and the inner thoughts in the soul that wonders about the mystery of life and what comes after it. It is a theology of misery, devoid of hope, and denies the very question that would reveal God to its adherents. This book will seek to unfold the questions that Christians and non-Christians have about eternal life, heaven, hell, the spirit-realm, and the new creation to come.

Now that we have an understanding of the Scriptural definition of eternal life, let's seek to answer what the Scriptures teach about what happens to people after they die. These answers regarding eternal life speak peace and hope to our souls in ways that empower us to live without fear of death while enjoying the human experience as we walk out our sojourn in this life.

The most wonderful revelation in Scripture is that human life possesses meaning, intrinsic value, and beauty amid a creation that is colored with death. Scripture reveals that eternal life transcends the death that colors this world and that eternal life is with God and being joined to Him in a covenant relationship that begins with His Son, Jesus Christ. The first Adam may have failed to maintain the glory of the original design, but the Second Adam, Jesus, prevailed and leads humanity towards the restoration of the original design as it unfolds in the time-space continuum.

CHAPTER 2

Wha† Happens When We Die?

"Yes, we are of good courage, and we would rather be away from the body and at home with the Lord."
2 Corinthians 5:8

As we survey the Scriptures on the subject of consciousness after death, we find that the Bible indicates that there is consciousness after physical death. Indeed, ancient cultures all over the globe have a hope of life after death as archeologists and sociologists have discovered after studying ancient cultures and civilizations. Eternity is written on the hearts of humanity by design, and this explains humanity's fascination with what is beyond the sojourn in this life when all the seasons of this life have expired. The Bible defines consciousness after this life in highly poetic language that we will survey and draw our conclusions from these verses.

The first section of Scripture we will explore will be Isaiah 14:9, "Sheol beneath is stirred up to meet you when you come; it rouses the shades to greet you, all who were leaders of the earth; it raises from their thrones all who were kings of the nations." This verse is referencing the judgment of God on the King of Babylon and his nation at some point in their future. Isaiah prophesied that Nebuchadnezzar would invade Judah, siege Jerusalem, destroy the Temple, and exile Judah. Isaiah then prophesies the Lord God would judge Babylon and as part of that judgment, the King of Babylon would be mocked by the dead in Sheol, the Old Testament designation for the abode of the dead. The section of verses in Isaiah 14:1-23 describes in typical Hebrew poetic hyperbole of God's vengeance on the injustices that Babylon meted out on Judah in the day of God's chastisement of Judah. Additionally, we also see a parallel reference to God's judgment of Satan (Lucifer) that will come at the end of this age when Messiah defeats all of His enemies, including death. This is truly a beautiful and hopeful passage that teaches us the Lord will bring victory, restoration, and justice to His people and judge the oppressors of His people. Isaiah 14:9 teaches us that after this life, there is immediate consciousness after the death of the physical body. There are other Old Testament passage we could look at, but Isaiah 14:1-23 is a clear passage that shows us people are conscious after death. It is also important to point out here that the verse references the wicked dead.

Another beautiful passage in the Old Testament Scripture that points to our hope of eternal life is Psalm 23:6 where David prophesies, "Surely goodness and mercy shall follow me all the days of my life, and I shall dwell in the house of the LORD forever." David points our attention to the expectation that life after death will be a reality that is wrapped in God's goodness and mercy for those who are the objects of His love. This is so very comforting because it gives us confidence in the Lord's ability to save us from the death of the body and bless us with an experience of bliss after our death. He truly is a Good Shepherd. The Hebrew text ties eternal life to God Himself. Our English translators use "forever" in our translations to bring out this truth. Psalm 23 is another glorious poetic text that teaches God's people should have an expectation of eternal life after the death of the physical body.

What Did Jesus Say About Life After Death?

The Old Testament uses poetic hyperbolic language to describe subjects like death, Sheol (Hell), the judgment of the dead, and the resurrection of the righteous. It is important to point this out because to draw conclusions from the text requires the interpreter to have an intimate knowledge of the Hebrew culture and the ancient East. Though the Old Testament Scriptures may be veiled concerning death and life after death, Jesus makes very definitive statements about these subjects.

In this section, we will look at the things Jesus says and learn from our glorious Risen Messiah. Because Jesus is the Son, the Second Person of the Trinity, so the things that He says are the very words of God and can be trustworthy, believable, and authoritative on any subject we desire to learn.

The first passage we will explore

is Matthew 17:1-8. In this passage, Jesus takes Peter, James, and John to a mountaintop where He reveals His glory to them in the Transfiguration. They were blessed to gaze on the glory of the uncreated Son who manifests His beauty, power, and glory to them. John hints about this experience in 1 John 1, as he writes to his spiritual children in Ephesus. Peter is more clear in 2 Peter 1:16-18, where he describes the experience as an apologetic for his readers to believe his testimony about Messiah, Jesus Christ. These three apostles heard the voice of the Father saying, "This is my beloved Son, with whom I am well pleased," and witnessed Jesus speaking with Elijah and Moses. Though Jesus does not say anything about eternal life directly in this passage, the unveiling of His glory and speaking with Elijah and Moses teaches us that there is life after the death of the physical body. Though these men are not resurrected, they are alive, conscious, recognizable, and capable of communicating. We should also see that these two men, Moses and Elijah, represent the Law and the Prophets who bear witness to Peter, James, and John that Jesus is the Messiah.

The next passage we will explore is Luke 19:19-31, where Jesus illustrates the nature of life after death in the story of the Rich Man and Lazarus. It is interesting to point out that though this narrative is found amid a few parables and teaching moments, Jesus seems to refer to Lazarus in language that indicates that He may have known Lazarus personally. Scholars tell us we have every reason to believe that Jesus is using an actual example of someone familiar with the Lord.

In the narrative, Jesus describes the life of Lazarus as a life of suffering and affliction, while the Rich Man enjoyed a life of feasting, wealth, and luxury. We have a contrast between the lives of the unrighteous who live in luxury and the oppressed who hope for their consolation in God. "Lazarus" is the Hellenized version of the proper Hebrew name, Eleazar which means "with the help of God," he is afflicted like Job, and the narrative points to the hope Lazarus has in his death, that he would enjoy grace and peace in the end. The contrast also points to the responsibility of the Rich Man to have cared for Lazarus and the narrative reveals the hardness of his heart in not fulfilling the Mosaic Law to care for the sick, poor, and oppressed of their people. Both of these men die a physical death in the narrative and end up alive in a spiritual reality after their deaths.

Lazarus is escorted by angels to a place that Jesus calls Abraham's Bosom. Abraham's Bosom was a spiritual reality where the righteous dead were consoled and comforted until the resurrection of Jesus Christ. In Ephesians 4:7-10, Paul alludes to this spiritual reality when he writes about the resurrection of Jesus, and Him freeing the righteous dead who were waiting for their entry to the very presence of God in Heaven when Jesus delivered them from Sheol.

Lazarus enjoys comfort next to the patriarch Abraham and is vindicated by God for his faith and hope in the comfort to come during his time of suffering at the rich man's gate. Notice that Abraham is also alive having the ministry of comforting the righteous dead in Sheol. Lazarus is blessed by God in his death in that has truly helped him as he enjoys life after death in the place of His goodness, waiting for the resurrection of the dead.

Though there is not much written about Abraham's Bosom in the Scriptures, the concept of a place where the righteous dead were comforted was an established belief in First Century Judaism. Since Jesus tells the narrative of the spiritual reality of Abraham's Bosom it should be believed as true.

Another term for this place where the righteous dead enjoy blessedness was called "paradise" in Jewish culture. In any case, Jesus affirms its existence and that in itself gives it legitimacy.

It is wonderful to note the righteous dead are never alone in their death because Lazarus was escorted by two angels to the place of comfort after his life in this realm. Jesus teaches us the righteous dead, like Lazarus, are alive after death, not alone, comforted, and blessed.

When we consider the Rich Man, we see that the unrighteous dead are alive and conscious after death and are segregated from the righteous dead. In this narrative, the righteous and the unrighteous were aware of each other's situations as the Rich Man sees that his state of life after death is not comforting but torment. The Greek word for "torment," **basanos** means "to be tested by a touchstone." It is a metaphor for being in pain, discomfort, or in a state of unbelief. This is the way Hades, the abode of the unrighteous dead, is described by Jesus. Jesus does not give us a graphic description of what type of torment the Rich Man endured, but we can deduce it is not a good place.

In the narrative, the Rich Man calls out to Abraham to ask for Lazarus to bring relief from his agony and the flame. It is so interesting that the Rich Man was asking for relief from the very one who laid at his gates suffering, needing relief in their lifetime. This is an illustration that God's justice will always prevail, either in this life or eternal life. It is difficult to determine the very nature of Hades from the narrative and if the Rich Man was suffering from a physical flame because the Greek word for "flame" can be used allegorically. What we can determine here is that whatever the burning is like, it is negative and the imagery in the narrative invokes a multitude of thoughts and feelings to the reader as a warning to live under the authority of God all the days of our lives.

As the story continues, Abraham reminds the Rich Man about the choices he has made to live in luxury during his life is all the comfort he would experience. The point of the Rich Man's life is that the pursuit of wealth and luxury without considering a godly life is the folly that led him to Hades, and is an example to others who choose the same.

Abraham continues answering the Rich Man by saying, "And besides all this, between us and you a great chasm has been fixed, so that those who would pass from here to you may not be able, and none may cross from there to us." Jesus gives us definitive information that the unrighteous dead and the righteous dead are not together. The spiritual chasm that separates them is fixed. This reveals to us that being unrighteous at the time of death is an irreversible consequence of a life of sin.

Rich Man then asks for Abraham to send Lazarus back from the dead to warn his five brothers about the consequences of a lifetime of sinful living. Abraham answers the Rich Man back that the brothers have Moses and the Prophets, or in other words, these five brothers have the witness of Scripture and the Word of God contains all the necessary information to obtain eternal life with God. The Rich Man continues and tells Abraham that if someone comes back from the dead, that people will listen to their witness. Abraham answers that if his brothers do not hear Moses and the Prophets they will be unconvinced that Hades is waiting for them.

It is in the story of the Rich Man and Lazarus, that Jesus gives us the most information about life after death. Through this narrative, we learn the righteous dead and the unrighteous dead are conscious after death, there is a separation between them, they are aware of their situations, either in bliss or in torment, and that the living has no contact with the dead because the dead cannot go back to the living.

The last Scripture we will look at here is Luke 23:32-43, when Jesus is being crucified between two thieves. Luke records that these thieves were mocking Jesus as He suffered for the sins of humanity. Jesus, Himself, bore the penalty for all sin which is, itself, death. During Jesus' suffering, one of the thieves realized his guilt and acknowledged Jesus' innocence. He looked at Jesus and somehow the need for grace moved his heart, so the thief asked Jesus to receive him at his death. Jesus replied, "Truly, I say to you, today you will be with me in paradise." This is such a powerful illustration of how the love of God and saving faith is extended to the sinner in the last moment of life, providing hope that it is never too late to acknowledge our sinfulness and be received into glory.

Though the example of the thief in Luke's gospel is not the major point, it stands as a powerful witness that there is life after this life. The demonstration of grace that is extended to the thief on the cross is a witness that salvation is not by works but by faith. The thief was neither baptized nor confirmed, he simply realized his sinful state, acknowledged Jesus' goodness and innocence, asked Jesus to be received, and Jesus confirmed the thief's acceptance by His answer. Salvation was by faith alone and paradise was granted to him. This short interaction in Luke 23:32-43 again shows that life after death is real and Jesus confirmed its reality as He forgave the thief and accepted him into glory.

Life After Death in The Epistles

The Apostle Paul mentions the hope of life after physical death in 2 Corinthians twice, and also once in 1 and 2 Thessalonians. In this section, we explore each one of these verses and draw conclusions from the text.

The first Scripture we will look at is 2 Corinthians 5:8, "Yes, we are of good courage, and we would rather be away from the body and at home with the Lord." Here, Paul is writing to the Corinthian Church to encourage them to stay true to Christ in the face of persecutions, and afflictions, because there is the reward of eternal life for those who endure to the end. Paul's exhortation begins in 2 Corinthians 5:1 and ends in verse 21.

This is a wonderful Scripture that speaks to us today about how living for Jesus in any circumstance carries eternal weight and glory and will be rewarded as we wait for Him either in His Second Coming or in our death. In 2 Corinthians 5:1, as inspired by the Holy Spirit, Paul wrote, "if our earthly tent is destroyed, we have a building from God." Later in verse eight, Paul states boldly that when we "depart from our human body we are present with the Lord." Notice that we do not have any intimate details as to what type of form we have after we die, but from the things that Jesus taught and what Paul writes, we can conclude that we are recognizable, have some contained form that mirrors our earthly form, and we are consciously alive.

Our next example of life in heaven is found in 2 Corinthians 12:1-4. Here, Paul writes about himself and describes an encounter that he had in defense of his apostolic ministry to the Corinthian Church who was questioning his authority as an apostle. In these verses, Paul describes being caught up to the third heaven, or paradise, and hearing or experiencing revelations that could not be spoken about. Though Paul did not say he died, he did enter God's realm, either in the body or outside the body, and witnessed God's perfect presence and everything that comes with that experience. Some scholars believe this occurred when Paul was stoned at Lystra in Acts 14. These scholars speculate that Paul died, went to the third heaven, and then returned to complete his ministry. Scripture does not say this directly, but it does not do violence to the text to believe this. Lastly, the third heaven in First Century Jewish theology was the place where the Godhead dwelled and manifested in perfection, glory, and beauty. This was Paul's context for writing about his experience, implying that there is a spiritual reality where life after death exists in a perfect place in the presence of the Godhead.

To clarify, the Old Testament and New Testament Scriptures describe three levels of heaven. The first being the created atmosphere that surrounds the earth. We see the first heaven referenced in the following Scriptures: Deuteronomy 11:17; 28:12, Judges 5:4, and Acts 14:17. The second heaven is outer space where we can reference the following Scriptures: Psalm 19:4, Jeremiah 8:2, and Isaiah 13:10. The third heaven is God's dwelling place and we can reference the following Scriptures: 1 Kings 8:30, Psalm 2:4, and Matthew 5:16. Regarding spiritual warfare and the activity of Satan and his demons, it seems from the Scripture that they are active and currently limited to the first and second heavens, not the third heaven since after the resurrection and ascension of Jesus Christ. There is so much that can be written about spiritual warfare, but we will save that for another book.

Our next section of Scripture is 1 Thessalonians 4:13-18. In these verses, Paul gives the Thessalonian Church comfort and hope in the face of persecution and death. He encourages all Christians to process grief in the context of hope in eternal life. This hope that Paul offers hinges around the truth that those who have died in Christ are with Him, coming with Him at the consummation of the kingdom of God, will be resurrected with a new body, and those Christians who have not died at the return of Jesus Christ will be transformed and caught up, and in an instant be changed to be like them. 1 Thessalonians 4:14 says, "For since we believe that Jesus died and rose again, even so, through Jesus, God will bring with him those who have fallen asleep." The implication in verse 14, is that the dead in Christ are already present with Jesus and they will return with Jesus as He is gloriously revealed by a loud command from heaven, the trumpet call of God, and the voice of the archangel. Paul is describing a dramatically beautiful and awe-inspiring picture of the revelation of Jesus Christ when He returns to judge the dead, renew creation, and inaugurate the eternal order. Christians everywhere in every age should hold onto this hopeful expectation of God's goodness in this life, in the intermediate state, and in the age to come.

The whole chapter of 2 Thessalonians 1, is not only an encouraging text for the Thessalonians who were being persecuted for their faith in Christ, but also for every generation of Christians who have had to endure persecution and death for the Name of Christ. Consciousness after death is not directly mentioned in the text, however, it is implied in verse10, "when he comes on that day to be glorified in his saints and to be marveled at among all who have believed because our testimony to you was believed."   This verse gives us hope, though implied, that the righteous dead are with Christ and will be glorified at His return and the enemies of Christ experience His vengeance for their persecutions against His Church and are eternally destroyed. Later in 2 Thessalonians 2:16, Paul writes about the eternal comfort we experience being with the Son and the Father in every season of our life. The implied hope in the text is that God's comfort is eternal, and because it is eternal, we who are in Christ experience His comfort in this life and after the death of the physical body. A person needs to be alive, to be eternally comforted.

The last example we will look at in the Apostolic Epistles is 2 Peter 1:11-14, which reads:

> "For in this way there will be richly provided for you an entrance into the eternal kingdom of our Lord and Savior Jesus Christ. Therefore, I intend always to remind you of these qualities, though you know them and are established in the truth that you have. I think it right, as long as I am in this body, to stir you up by way of a reminder since I know that the putting off of my body will be soon, as our Lord Jesus Christ made clear to me."

Peter mentions our "entrance into the eternal kingdom" for living a life of faith in Christ Jesus. He then goes on to mention his impending death and seeks to impart as much encouragement and exhortation that he can before he is martyred by Nero. Though

Peter does not mention immediate consciousness after death, he certainly writes with confidence that he will experience the eternal kingdom after he is dead. This revelation came directly from Jesus to Peter and he is confident in the consolation that waits for him.

The apostolic expectation of life after death is taught in the New Testament Epistles. Both Paul and Peter believed this and encouraged the Christian communities they fathered to have hope in a life that will always be. Christians in every epoch of history have found their comfort from Scripture as they were persecuted and grieved the loss of loved ones. They even found comfort in the aging process that there is a glorious hope of life after death, a resurrection body to come, and an eternal kingdom of God, lit by His very presence. The book of Revelation gives us even more direct details of immediate consciousness after death.

In the next section, we will look at some passages from Revelation that give us undeniable evidence of consciousness after death.

Consciousness After Death In Revelation

The book of Revelation gives us dramatic scenes of the righteous dead worshipping the Godhead, adoring and praising the glorified Jesus Christ, as well as crying out for God to avenge those who were persecuted and martyred for Jesus. Revelation 6:9-11 contains fantastic imagery of the souls of believers who have been martyred, alive, under the altar of God, crying out for the Lord to avenge their blood. The Lord comforts them, clothes them in white, and gives them rest while they wait. In other scenes, particularly Revelation 7:9-17, John gives us intimate details of the righteous dead praising the Godhead, glorifying the Lamb (Jesus our Passover), in concert with the four living creatures, the twenty-four elders, and the angels surrounding the throne. These sections of Scripture in Revelation invite our minds to wander into the mystery, glory, and power of the Holy Trinity and encourage us that what waits for us after this life is nothing less than the indescribable worship and experiential knowledge of the Person of God. This is the beauty of the Revelation: the unfolding of God's beauty, His power, and His dominion that is and will be on earth as human history moves towards its restoration and redemption of the cosmos.

The book of Revelation is truly a revelation of hope that strengthened the Early Church to endure the spiritual battles for the dominion of the gospel of Jesus Christ over the dominion of darkness and to be comforted knowing that in all things, Jesus is their Lord. Even to their deaths, Christians of every age have placed their hope in the dominion that is in Christ which will someday be unveiled at His Second Coming. The book of Revelation outlines the cosmic

spiritual warfare that is being victori-
ously waged against the serpent and
his seed, by the Church, and by Christ,
obtaining the ultimate victory which is
the destruction of Hades and death
itself.

What About The Great Cloud of Witnesses?

Unfortunately in Charismatic
circles, a theology of the active par-
ticipation of the righteous dead in the
life of the believer on earth is emerging. It is a re-spin of the medieval
theology of intercession by the saints
and makes an opportunity for Christians
to minimize their direct and wonderful
relationship with the Holy Trinity. My
observation in the context of the
modern Charismatic Movement has
been to place the importance of
personal revelations over the sure
tutor of the Scriptures, that are inspired
by the Holy Spirit Himself, and are the
clearest source of information about
God and our experiences with Him.
As a passionate charismatic Christian,

I affirm and promote mystical spiritual experiences, spiritual gifts from the Holy Spirit, the baptism of the Holy Spirit, signs and wonders, and the importance of prophecy in the lives of all believers. However, as a committed scholar and theologian to Scriptural truth and revelation, I will always speak up about ancient heresies that re-emerge in our era of Church history. It seems that the modern Charismatic Movement is fertile ground for new teachings and revelations that stand at odds with Biblical truth, the ancient and historical confessions of the Universal Church, and the Christian orthodoxy.

The great revivalist John Wesley developed the Wesleyan Quadrilateral which remains relevant today and is a wonderful tool that helps charismatic Christians maintain truth in the midst of experiencing spiritual phenomena. Every Pentecostal and Charismatic Christian should be thankful for the great theology of the Wesleyan Movement which set up the foundation for the Azusa Street Revival in the early 20th century. If it was not for the Wesleyan Movement's teaching of the second grace of the Holy Spirit after conversion, then hungry Christians in that era would not have had the encouragement to partner with the Holy Spirit and pursue the baptism of the Holy Spirit and the spiritual gifts.

The Wesleyan Quadrilateral revolves around processing our personal beliefs and spiritual experiences through four metrics of evaluation. These are Scripture, Tradition, Reason, and Experience. This is an easy way to process teachings we might hear and spiritual experiences we might have, so that we may stay in orthodoxy and not stray from the faith or mislead other Christians because of our passion, ignorance, or even discern when we are being deceived by false teachers. During his ministry, John Wesley experienced various "enthusiasms" or manifestations that ranged from the mild to the wild. This made the opportunity for many of his critics to ridicule what God was doing through his revival movement. These revival meeting manifestations eventually led the Wesleyan Movement to develop a framework for maturing their movement without quenching the Holy Spirit. Again, the Quadrilateral is still a great tool for Spirit-filled Christians to use to stay in truth without discounting personal spiritual experiences or spiritual manifestations in our meetings. I encourage all Charismatic Christians to study the Wesleyan Quadrilateral and begin to filter their positions and spiritual experiences through it. It will be of great benefit to the modern Charismatic Movement to begin to embrace spiritual maturity and sound Biblical orthodoxy.

The Great Cloud of Witnesses passage is found in Hebrews 12:1-2. Let's read the text and see what it says:

> "Therefore, since we are surrounded by so great a cloud of witnesses, let us also lay aside

every weight, and the sin which clings so closely, and let us run with endurance the race that is set before us, looking to Jesus, the founder and perfecter of our faith, who for the joy that was set before him endured the cross, despising the shame, and is seated at the right hand of the throne of God."

To understand any text, we need to consider the context of the verses. Previously in Hebrews 11, the writer gives a list of examples of people of God who lived by faith, believed God, hoped for the Messiah, and maintained their vision for another age that was prophesied and eventually realized in the incarnation of Jesus Christ. The whole book of Hebrews is an exhortation for Messianic believers in the First Century not to abandon their Messianic Christianity in the face of Jewish persecution and return to Law-keeping and Temple worship.

Hebrews 11 is an awe-inspiring section of the Scripture that unveils the glory and power of living in faith with Christ. It is a glorious manifesto that releases courage and boldness to any believer who reads it. As Hebrews 11 ends, the writer sums up the exhortation in Hebrews 12:1-2 with a "therefore," continuing to explain and encourage just how important it is to remain faithful to our Lord Jesus in every season of life, every circumstance, and to endure and receive our unshakable eternal kingdom of God that is promised to all who believe.

The Great Cloud of Witnesses that the writer makes mention of in Hebrews 12:1 surrounds the Church and refers to the people in Hebrews 11 that we can use as examples of those who finished well and received glory from God. The Greek word for "surrounded" is **perikei-mai**. It means "to be compassed with;" meaning that Scripture provides us with various narratives of people of faith to inspire us as we live out our journey here by faith. The writer is exhorting every Christian that the history of our faith is full of examples of people who lived before us and who are written about in Scripture as a way to encourage our faithful pursuit of Christ and finish well in this life. It is not saying that these witnesses are cheering us on or are even aware of our situations during our sojourn here on earth.

The main encouragement in the text is to lay aside the sin that prevents us from finishing well with God, laying aside our burdens and placing our trust in Christ, and finally moving in the grace of endurance throughout our whole Christian life. The thought is, if the faithful people in Hebrews 11 persevered, then we, too, can persevere by meditating on their lives, considering their faithful examples, and applying the lessons of their examples to our lives today. The Old Testament faithful anticipated the arrival of the Messiah and looked forward to His revelation. The New Covenant believers look to the past to be inspired and strengthen themselves so that we might live for Christ every day as we wait for His return. This is the revelation and main thrust of the Great Cloud of Witnesses section of Scripture.

Lastly, I would remind us that Jesus teaches in the narrative of the Rich Man and Lazarus that the righteous and un-righteous dead cannot communicate with the living. They have lived their lives and have completed their sojourn and we have ours to live in faithfulness to Christ. The landing point is that the Great Cloud of Witnesses obtained heaven by their faith and faith-filled living as they trusted God in all things. Now that we have their example, we should do the same.

What Happens to Us When We Die?

The Scriptures are clear that all people, whether they are in a relation-ship with God through Jesus Christ or are not in a relationship with Jesus Christ, experience consciousness after they die. The people who are made righteous by the goodness of grace in the blood of Christ are enveloped in bliss and comfort. The people who are not in a relationship with God through Jesus Christ are waiting in Hades/Hell/Sheol for the general resurrection of the dead, the Great White Throne judgment, and finally, the penalty of eternal death.

In the next chapter, we will explore the details of what happens to the unrighteous dead and after that, address what happens to our physical bodies at the resurrection.

CHAPTER 3

Wha† Happens †o †he Unrighteous Dead?

"And the sea gave up the dead who were in it,
Death and Hades gave up the dead who were in them,
and they were judged, each one of them,
according to what they had done."
Revelation 20:13

In Chapter Two, we explored a few sections of Scripture that taught us that both the righteous and the unrighteous dead are conscious after death and experiencing bliss or discomfort, depending on their responses to the grace of God in Jesus Christ. The righteous are in heaven and the unrighteous are in Hades/Sheol/Hell.

When we consider what happens to the unrighteous dead, we should first look to Scripture and then we should approach this subject with grace, mercy, and an awareness that is void of spiritual pride, judgment, a spirit of religion, or self-righteousness. The subject is about the eternal destinies of people, the very serious judgment of God, and the reality that all people who are saved are dependent on God's grace and mercy in terms of their standing before Him. There is no one perfect except the Perfect One, Jesus Christ, the only perfect Son of Man and Son of God. It is so important to always tell the truth in a spirit of love, concern, and care when theologians approach subjects like Hades, judgment, and the eternal destruction of the sinner.

In my last book, *Diakrino: How is God Judging the World Today?*, I looked at the five expressions of God's judgment in Scripture. One of those judgments is the judgment of hell. In Christian history, there have been three beliefs that have emerged about the judgment of hell. These three positions are Universalism, Eternal Conscious Torment, and Evangelical Conditionalism. I will define them below to bring clarity to each position so that we can understand what Christians have believed about the judgment of hell.

Universalism

The universalist view was popularized by the early church father Origen and has never been a majority view in historic Christianity. This view stands on the following theological positions: all souls are immortal, saint or sinner, Jesus' sacrifice on Calvary redeems every person's sin and saves them whether they have accepted Jesus' gift of salvation in the gospel or not, and finally, the fires of hell are remedial in nature and every unbeliever will be "purified" by the fires of hell and eventually all people will bend the knee to Christ and be saved and live with Him eternally.

Again, this view is not a majority view and faces many difficulties when trying to build a Biblical apologetic for it. Though there is more interest in the universalist view of hell today, it lacks any strong Biblical precedent and has struggled for formal recognition within the wider family of Christian theology. Many would say that this view undermines the call to live as a committed disciple of Christ, engage in the sanctification process of becoming more like Him, encourages libertine living, and opens the door to accept amoral thinking in the greater Christian ethos of a culture. However, the view is optimistic in the way it sees the unrighteous dead and is emerging as a popular position now that Western society and culture are drifting to a more humanistic worldview, leaving the Judeo-Christian ethos of classical Western culture and worldview.

Eternal Conscious Torment

The eternal conscious torment view of hell became popularized in the 3rd Century AD as the most common view of Christians through the Middle Ages to the Reformation and is now the majority view in the Modern Era. The early church father, Augustine popularized the eternal conscious torment view in his book, *The City of God*, and this is the predominant view of most Christians of all denominations, faith traditions, or movements in modern Christianity. This view is sometimes called the Traditionalist view of hell. This view stands on three theological positions: the souls of all people are immortal, sinner or saint, Hell is the everlasting, eternal suffering and torment of the sinner and finally, the wages of sin is death. However, the concept of death is not understood in its natural meaning of the word, but death becomes a metaphor that describes the quality of eternal life for the sinner in hell. A reality that the traditionalist says, ceases to be human and is therefore a typology of death, not a literal death. Both universalism and the eternal conscious torment view are built around a Platonic construct of the cosmos and are rooted in the ideals of Classical Greek philosophy which beliefs in the immortality of the soul.

Evangelical Conditionalism

The conditionalist view of hell which emerged in early Christian history, only to fade in popularity in the third and fourth centuries, is now enjoying a resurgence in evangelical Christianity. Again, the conditionalist view stands on three theological positions: immortality of the soul is a gift from God and is only given when a person is in the right relationship with God, the wages of sin is death to the offender, and the fires of hell punish the sinner according to their degree of sin and the sinner will ultimately be burned out of existence. This judgment is irreversible and eternal.

Evangelical Conditionalism is currently a minority view that is being revisited by many evangelical Christians who wrestle with reconciling the goodness of God with the doctrine of hell or final judgment. Their argument for conditionalism questions whether it is congruent with God's nature and character to punish a soul in eternal conscious torment for a limited lifetime of sin.

There are metaphors in Scripture that describe the length of human life as a vapor, a mist, a fading flower, or like grass. If Scripture describes human life in such temporal terms, then conditionalists argue that the eternal conscious torment of the sinner for 70-120 years of sinful living is not congruent with the eternal, pure, good, and holy nature of God. It is refreshing to see that there has been a resurgence of this view with modern Christian theologians and scholars that are seeking to rediscover early Christian thoughts and teachings on subjects like Hell/Hades/Sheol.

The conditionalist view of hell bases its worldview in the Hebrew construct of the cosmos and does not read any other worldview, like Platonism into the text. While there are many great scholars on all sides of the positions regarding the judgment of hell, the conditionalist camp is re-thinking the popular eternal conscious torment view through the discipline of hermeneutics, cultural studies, and statements by the Early Church Fathers and through that academic pursuit, theologians like myself are finding themselves adopting the conditionalist position on the doctrine of hell.

All the great reformations of the Christian faith have three things in common. First, they all look to Scripture as the foundation of belief through an intellectually honest examination of the text. Second, they challenge the current Christian orthopraxy and ask pointed questions. Third, reformations in Christianity have been led by bold Christians that are committed to the truth and are unafraid of the fallout of being excommunicated or martyred for that truth.

We have the examples of Martin Luther, John Huss, John Calvin, John Wesley, Madam Guyon, Aimee Semple-McPhearson, and William Seymour who irrevocably changed the expression of Christianity in their life-times. These reformers did not discover new revelation but discovered buried Biblical truth, veiled on the pages of Scripture, veiled by history, but revealed by the Holy Spirit and a witness and practice in the Early Church.

It is my position that the con-ditionalist view of hell is the most Scriptural view of hell, historically congruent to the beliefs of the Early Church. I believe it will be one of the last reformations of the Christian Church next to the emergence of the 5-Fold Offices of apostle, prophet, evangelist, pastor, and teacher. It is my hope that you, dear reader, will take the time to re-think the doctrine of hell and search out the conditionalist position like the Bereans before us.

The prospect of the judgment of hell is a doctrine that all Christians have considered when we reflect on the sacrificial death of Jesus on the cross. We believe that Jesus died on the cross as the only true, and one sacrifice for sin and that the penalty of our sin was reconciled with God through that one act. Every Christian believes that they are saved from the eternal judgment of hell by the blood of Christ and trust in His sacrifice on the cross as the sacrifice that saves us from that fate. The judgment of hell is the personal accountability of the individual sinner to stand before a holy and perfect God, give an account of their lives, and receive the just penalty for their offenses against God's moral law in the light of His Person. The judgment of hell reveals the goodness and grace of God as much as it reveals His justice.

May we all look at the judgment of hell with hearts of gratitude knowing that we have been saved from this horrifying fate! The cross opens our hearts to the terrifying reality of hell because Jesus demonstrated the penalty of sin as He suffered on the cross. The metaphor for hell was revealed on the cross.

The remainder of this chapter will explore the resurrection of the unrighteous dead, the Biblical metaphors for the end of the sinner, and an examination of the conditionalist view of hell.

The Resurrection of the Unrighteous Dead

Now that these three views of hell have been defined it is time to look at what Scripture has to say about the resurrection of the unrighteous dead and their end. Scripture teaches that the physical body is laid to rest in the dust and the souls of the unrighteous dead and the souls and spirits of the righteous dead are conscious after death. Genesis 3:19, Job 20:11, Daniel

12:2, and Ecclesiastes 12:7 all support the thought that the physical body decays and rests in the dust while the spirit/soul lives on in an intermediate state where the saint or the sinner waits for either the resurrection of eternal life in a renewed creation of eternal destruction.

Jesus said in John 5:28-29, "Do not marvel at this, for an hour is coming when all who are in the tombs will hear his voice and come out, those who have done good to the resurrection of life, and those who have done evil to the resurrection of judgment." Jesus taught that the physical body will be resurrected and after the resurrection we are to face accountability for the way we lived our lives. It is a sobering thought to live with an awareness that our daily decisions carry an eternal witness. It reminds us that all life carries eternal dimensions of either grace and mercy in Christ, or judgment, trial, and death for the rebellious.

At the end of the age, the soul and body of the sinner are reunited, stand before Jesus Christ, and then experience what the Bible calls the "second death." The second death language is used in four places: Revelation 2:11; 20:6; 20:14; and 21:8. The most graphic verse is Revelation 21:8, "But as for the cowardly, the faithless, the detestable, as for murderers, the sexually immoral, sorcerers, idolaters, and all liars, their portion will be in the lake that burns with fire and sulfur, which is the second death." The first death is the death of the physical body and the second death is the eternal death that comes after the judgment. The Scriptures teach that the wages of sin is death and we see this in graphic imagery in the book of Revelation.

As we conclude this section, Jesus also described the unbelieving as "spiritually dead" when He interacted with the scribe who made an excuse not to follow Jesus in Matthew 8:18-22. It is here Jesus says, "Follow me, and leave the dead to bury their dead." The implication in the text is that those who are not disciples of Christ are spiritually dead. Jesus said that He was the Life for all life comes from Him and He is the grace-filled Messiah who is the resurrection and holds the keys of death and Hades. When we read Revelation 21:8 we all can see ourselves in the text and that should move our hearts to gratitude and worship towards God because of the goodness that has covered these sins by the blood of the Lamb.

What About Those Who Have Never Heard?

It is an interesting thought to consider the fates of those who have never heard the gospel of Jesus Christ. It was for God's great love for humanity that He promised Messiah after the Fall in Eden and then unfolded the promise through the covenants that He made with humanity, and with Israel being the witness of His unfathomable power and loving-kindness to the Gentile world. God has always looked at the world with a Fatherly redemptive vision of Eden lost to Eden restored. There is one passage in Scripture that speaks of humanity being accountable to the revelation that they have given and makes a provision for God to show mercy to a person who has never heard the gospel. It is Romans 2:12-16:

> "For all who have sinned without the law will also perish without the law, and all who have sinned under the law will be judged by the law. For it is not the hearers of the law who are righteous before God, but the doers of the law who will be justified. For when Gentiles, who do not have the law, by nature do what the law requires, they are a law to themselves, even though they do not have the law. They show that the work of the law is written on their hearts, while their conscience also bears

witness, and their conflicting thoughts accuse or even excuse them on that day when, according to my gospel, God judges the secrets of men by Christ Jesus."

Certainly, Romans 1 makes the case that creation is a powerful revelation of the existence of God, and His power and majesty that would cause the whole aggregate of humanity to turn their hearts to Him. The text even goes so far as to say that humanity has no excuse for turning to idols and creating gods in the image of the creation. However, this text in Romans 2:12-16, gives space for God to give an exception for those who recognized His moral purity and respond to that revelation.

All humans are made in the image of God, therefore the inner-witness of the law is written on our hearts. A sense of right and wrong, morality, and justice is present in all cultures as a witness of the unique place that humanity holds in God's creation. We can conclude that Jesus is a Judge who knows the secrets of the human heart and only He can ultimately decide God's justice in the judgment regarding the conduct of those who have never heard the gospel of Jesus Christ.

In Acts 17, the Apostle Paul addresses the Areopagus in Athens and says, "The times of ignorance God overlooked, but now he commands all people everywhere to repent." We can imply without doing violence to the text that somehow and in some way God grants mercy in unique situations and those who have never heard may be judged based on the revelation they do have. However, once the gospel is proclaimed all possibilities of mercy in ignorance are removed. Christians need to have answers for these types of questions and trust the nature and character of God, which is an indescribable perfect moral beauty displayed in its fullness in Jesus Christ. This is an additional apolo-

getic for the Evangelical Conditionalist
view of hell.

The Great White Throne

The resurrection of the unrighteous
dead ushers in the judgment of the
Lamb before the Great White Throne.
This is evident in Revelation 20:11-15
which states:

> "Then I saw a great white throne
> and him who was seated on it.
> From his presence, earth and
> sky fled away, and no place
> was found for them. And I saw
> the dead, great and small,
> standing before the throne,
> and books were opened. Then
> another book was opened,
> which is the book of life. And
> the dead were judged by
> what was written in the books,
> according to what they had
> done. And the sea gave up
> the dead who were in it, Death
> and Hades gave up the dead
> who were in them, and they

were judged, each one of them, according to what they had done. Then Death and Hades were thrown into the lake of fire. This is the second death, the lake of fire. And if anyone's name was not found written in the book of life, he was thrown into the lake of fire."

Here we have in graphic detail the end of the unrighteous dead. The whole created order is uncovered and nothing is hidden from the presence of the Godhead and the dead bodies of all are resurrected, reunited with the soul, and judged according to all they have done. Hades is empty and those who are not written into the Lamb's book of life are cast into the lake of fire, and die the second death.

Seemingly, Revelation 20:11-15 gives us a play-by-play on the end of the unrighteous dead. It is at this point that it could be seen that

Universalism and the eternal conscious torment of the sinner doctrines of the judgment of hell fall apart: First, there are unrighteous dead that are judged and die the second death. Second, Death and Hades are destroyed in the lake of fire.

From the language in the text, it is implied that the lake of fire consumes what is cast into it. The lake of fire is a terrible consequence of living as a rebel against the God of mercy, loving-kindness, goodness, love, salvation, and any other good thing that can be imputed to the Holy Trinity. The very thought of being questioned by the Creator, giving an account for my life, and then being judged and cast into the lake of fire is unthinkable in terms of fear. If the whole of heaven is moved by the very glorious presence of God in reverence of Him, then imagine the reaction of mortal men and women will have when they come face to face with the One. Jesus said in Matthew 10:28, "Fear the One who can destroy both the soul and the body in hell."

Archetypes of the End of the Sinner

Revelation 20:11-15 describes a final and irreversible judgment of the wicked at the end of this world when all people are resurrected and give an account for their lives before God. The Scriptures give us information that describes the nature of the judgment of hell in a general sense. Below we will look at the common Scriptural metaphors and archetypes that help us understand the serious and sobering final judgment of the wicked in hell.

For the person who comes to accept the conditionalist position of the judgment of hell, hell is a revelation of God's justice and His mercy. Justice in the sense that sin is truly punished after a time in the sequester of Hades and then in a terrifying reality of a face-to-face encounter with God that ends in being cast into the lake of fire to be consumed. It is mercy from God because His goodness grants the grace of death for the offense of sin in the finality of the type of judgment that sinners receive in the lake of fire which is irreversible destruction.

Blown Away like Smoke and Melted like Wax

Psalm 68:1-2 describes the end of the wicked using the metaphor, "melted like wax." Psalm 68:1-2, "God shall arise, his enemies shall be scattered, and those who hate him shall flee before him! As smoke is driven away, so you shall drive them away; as wax melts before the fire, so the wicked shall perish before God!"

Psalm 68:1-2 also gives the reader various word pictures that teach us that rebellion against God is very serious and will end in a final, inescapable way. Though the wicked flee from the presence of the Lord, they are blown away like smoke and melted like wax. These metaphors describe the end of the wicked and teach us that the wicked have no strength or ability to flee, or resist;they will be "like smoke, like wax that melts" and this judgment from God is final and permanent. This type of language is similar to the language use in Revelation 20:11-15 which describes the irreversible destruction of the sinner. It is eternal because it cannot be reversed.

Consumed

One of the earliest metaphors for the final judgment of the wicked is found in Job 4:9. Job 4:9 reads, "By the breath of God they perish, and by the blast of his anger they are consumed." Other texts use this same metaphor or archetype for the final judgment of the sinner. These are Job 20:26, Psalm 104:35, Isaiah 1:28, and Jeremiah 9:16.

The Hebrew word translated "consumed" is **kalah**, which can mean "come to an end, be ended, finished, be destroyed, be used up, exterminated, or fail." The Hebrew word for "consumed" does not give any detailed information on what "consumed" is exactly, but it does give us enough information to know that the final judgment of the wicked is permanent and irreversible. It invokes a feeling of sobering accountability to God as one considers that one cannot run away, escape, or preserve their own life in God's presence. The "breath of God," indicates that life comes from Him and every person is accountable to God for their lives. Undoubtedly, we can conclude that if a person is not pleasing to God, they are "consumed"; their fate cannot be escaped and it is final.

The Wicked Die

Another description of the end of the wicked is death. This description is used in both the Old Testament and New Testament Scriptures. Before we explore Proverbs 11:19 and Romans 6:23, it is worthwhile to note that death is also used as a description for the end of the sinner in Proverbs 19:16, and Isaiah 22:18.

According to Proverbs 11:19, "Whoever is steadfast in righteousness will live, but he who pursues evil will die." The Proverbs are beautiful compressed parables that impart to us deep truths for life in their contrasts. Verses that use Hebrew parallelism are glorious because they are easy to memorize and give us wisdom that guides the course of our lives every day. The movements in Proverbs 11:19 are simple. The righteous live and the people that pursue evil die. The Hebrew word for "die" in Proverbs 11:19 is **maveth**. It means "to die, death, dying, death personified, the realm of the dead, death by violence, and death as a penalty." Though this text does not give us specifics on hell, it does teach us that the end of the sinner is death and not life, it is irreversible and final in its nature, which fits into the Revelation 20:11-15 description of the end of the wicked.

The next text that we will explore is Romans 6:23. It states, "For the wages of sin is death, but the gift of God is eternal life in Christ Jesus our Lord." In plain language, Romans 6:23 gives us two movements in the text that describe the end of the sinner. The first movement is that the payment for sin is death. The Greek word for "death" in the text is **thanatos**, which means "the death of the body, or separation of the soul from the body." The Strong's concordance expounds the definition to include "eternal conscious torment of the soul in the misery of hell," however, this definition of the word is expounded by the centuries of Christian tradition and not its etymology in Greek. The original use of the Greek word was simply "the death of the body."

Depending on the position of hell we hold, Romans 6:23 teaches us that death is not life. It is the just and final payment for the total of sinful choices that a person has made throughout their lifetimes. The plain meaning of any word in a written text is typically the easiest way to interpret that text.

The Wicked are Blown Away like Chaff

In Psalm 35:5, we find yet another metaphor for the final judgment of the wicked. Psalm 35:5 states, "Blow them away like chaff in the wind — a wind sent by the angel of the LORD." Other places in the Scriptures that use this word picture are Isaiah 29:5 and Hosea 13:3.

The metaphor of the wicked being "blown away like chaff" gives us very little detailed information concerning the final judgment other than the wicked will be removed like chaff is blown away by the wind. The imagery in the text teaches us that the wicked cannot resist the wind like chaff cannot resist the wind and that they will be removed and not recovered. Again, such a metaphor leads us to believe that the end of the wicked is final, irresistible, and irreversible.

Cut Off

One of the more common metaphors for the end of the wicked is that they are "cut off." Some of the Scriptures that use this metaphor are Job 24:24, Psalm 75:10; 34:16, and Isaiah 29:20. Let's explore Job 24:24 and look at this metaphor in detail. According to Job 24:24, "They are exalted a little while, and then are gone; they are brought low and gathered up like all others; they are cut off like the heads of grain."

There are several movements in the text that describe the end of the wicked. The first movement in the text is that the wicked only prosper for short time. Their prosperity and perceived quality of life are not permanent but temporal. The second movement indicates that they are removed from the presence of the righteous. The third movement goes on to explain that the wicked are humbled and have no strength to continue, while the fourth movement indicates that the wicked are gathered. The final movement in the text is that the wicked are cut off. The word for "cut off" in Hebrew is namal which means "to be circumcised, be clipped, or cut off." The archetype of being "cut off" contains a sense of permanence that is irreversible and final.

Burned like Chaff

John the Baptist describes the end of the wicked as being "burned up like chaff" and adds to the Old Testament imagery that agrees with the idea of an irresistible, irreversible and permanent end of the wicked for their sinful and evil ways. These examples are found in Matthew 3:12 and Luke 3:17:

> Matthew 3:12 - "His winnowing fork is in his hand, and he will clear his threshing floor and gather his wheat into the barn, but the chaff he will burn with unquenchable fire."

> Luke 3:17 - "His winnowing fork

is in his hand, to clear his threshing floor and to gather the wheat into his barn, but the chaff he will burn with unquenchable fire."

John's description of the end of the wicked adds a Messianic dimension to the final punishment of the wicked. "His winnowing fork" is an obvious reference to Jesus Christ who will stand as Judge of the living and the dead.

Look at the movements in the text. The first movement is that Jesus has the authority to judge the wicked since He holds the winnowing fork. The second movement shows that Jesus gathers the wheat. The wheat is what is good, therefore Jesus gathers the righteous. The third movement indicates that the wicked are burned with a fire that cannot be quenched, be put out or resisted; it is a fire that completely burns! John's description of the end of the wicked follows the

Old Testament themes of the final punishment of the wicked and adds the Messianic dimension of Messiah as the Judge who will execute the judgment of hell. These types and shadows in the text are expounded upon when we consider the description of the movements in Revelation 20:11-15.

Where the Worm does not Die

Jesus taught about the end of the wicked in His teachings, so it is important to review what Jesus said about the final judgment of hell. Jesus is the Word of God, so the statements that Jesus says and teaches are authoritative and must be believed. Jesus describes the end of the wicked or hell as a place where the "worm does not die, a fire that burns, and a place of weeping and gnashing of teeth." In this section, we will examine these metaphors and expand the information we have about the judgment of hell.

Jesus quoted Isaiah 66:24 in His

teachings on hell. This verse describes the end of the wicked at the end of the age. Isaiah 66:24 reads, "And they shall go out and look on the dead bodies of the men who have rebelled against me. For their worm shall not die, their fire shall not be quenched, and they shall be an abhorrence to all flesh." Jesus affirms the prophet Isaiah and confirms the veracity of Isaiah's prophecy of Scripture. It is important to see that Jesus never corrected the text of the Old Testament but affirmed it in every way. Jesus only corrected the misapplication of God's Word by the Sadducees and Pharisees.

Jesus quotes this verse from Isaiah in Mark 9:47-48. It reads, "And if your eye causes you to sin, tear it out. It is better for you to enter the kingdom of God with one eye than with two eyes to be thrown into hell, where their worm does not die and the fire is not quenched.'" For us to understand this verse, we need to consider the context of the culture that Jesus was speaking to. Jesus uses the Greek word **geena** or **Gehenna** (Hebrew) in the text. Gehenna is a metaphor for hell or the archetype for the "end of the wicked." It is the dump outside of Jerusalem where the carcasses of animals, trash, and the filth of the city were burned. It is located in the valley of Hinnom, south of Jerusalem. That was the place that Isaiah was referencing in Isaiah 66:24 and it is also the place that Jesus is referencing in Mark 47-48.

Gehenna, or Hinnom, was regularly burning the refuse, as also the maggots continuously fed on the dead flesh. The imagery in the text shows that whatever is put in hell is consumed by fire and maggots. We learn here the wicked are like useless refuse that is gathered, burned and eaten by worms in the Valley of Hinnom, and that the end of the wicked is permanent.

Weeping and Gnashing of Teeth

Another metaphor or archetype that Jesus uses in the Gospels is "weeping and gnashing of teeth" to describe the end of the wicked. The Scriptures where Jesus uses this metaphor are: Matthew 8:12; 13:42; 13:50; 22:13; 24:51; 25:30, and Luke 13:28. The imagery of "weeping and gnashing of teeth" is a reoccurring theme for the end of the wicked. It helps us expand our knowledge of the type of end the wicked will suffer. Let's look at Luke 13:28 and Matthew 25:30 as examples of Jesus using the "weeping and gnashing of teeth" metaphor:

> Luke 13:18 - "In that place, there will be weeping and gnashing of teeth, when you see Abraham and Isaac and Jacob and all the prophets in the kingdom of God but you cast out."

> Matthew 25:30 - "And cast the worthless servant into the outer darkness. In that place, there will be weeping and gnashing of teeth."

The text in Luke describes a "place" and the text in Matthew gives a description of that place as "outer darkness." The Greek words that describe the "outer darkness" that Jesus references are **exōteros skotos**. The literal meaning of these words is "outside darkness." **Skotos** in Greek is a metaphor for being "darkened in your thinking, under the influence of evil, or being devoid of the illuminating knowledge of God, or the light of God." The thought in the text is that the place where the wicked meet their end is a place devoid of the light of Messiah, Jesus Christ. The response of the wicked in the place where they are judged is weeping, synonymous with regret, or gnashing of teeth, synonymous with anger and rebellion. We learn that the righteous are gathered and enjoy the presence of Jesus and the wicked are cast out from His illuminating presence.

Jesus said He is the Resurrection and the Life. Without the presence of Jesus, there is only death. We have definitive information regarding the nature of hell, in that we know the wicked cannot resist Messiah's judgment and that they either weep with regret, or gnash their teeth in anger with rebellion at their end. Again, their end is irresistible, irreversible, and permanent in nature.

The souls of the wicked dead wait in Hades for the final judgment in an intermediate state. When Jesus returns they are resurrected and reunited with their physical bodies. They are then judged by the Lord face to face, and finally cast into the lake of fire to be consumed.

Can The Living Communicate with the Dead?

The clearest teaching we have in Scripture is the story Jesus tells about the Rich Man and Lazarus regarding whether the dead can communicate with the living. Since Jesus is the Word of God incarnate, the Walking Torah, we can take His word to be the irrefutable truth. From that narrative, the dead cannot communicate with the living. What about ghosts and people who say that they talk to the dead? What are we to believe regarding these types of paranormal and illegal supernatural activities? The best way to solve any spiritual mystery is to seek the answers in Scripture since it is God's very Word, trustworthy, and His very own revelation that gives us the answers He desires for each one of us.

The first command in Scripture regarding this is to never seek to consult the dead. In Leviticus 20:27, and Deuteronomy 18:9-14 the Lord commands His people to not consult anyone who seeks to speak to the dead. The Scripture tells us that this was one of the reasons the nations who possessed the Promised Land were being judged and driven out before the Israelites. The thought here is that our God speaks to His people directly in a relational way that is very personal in the context of an authentic relationship. The Lord makes a complaint against Judah, through Isaiah, in Isaiah 8:19 when the Lord says, "Why consult the dead on behalf of the living?" At that time they had neglected the Lord as their source of revelation for the issues of life.

In the Law, it declares those who are necromancers, astrologists, mediums, and those who practice witchcraft are worthy of death. This is because this type of sin denies that God is the fountainhead of revelation and leads us astray from the safety of spiritual phenomena and mystical experiences through the agency of the Holy Spirit. We are not to harm modern day spiritists because we know that the wages of sin are death, and we live in a New Covenant age where we are charged with proclaiming forgiveness and restoration in Christ. In the New Covenant age, God's people operate in grace and love, while we wait for His return. Christian spiritual phenomena and mystical experiences are for the greater glory and maturity of the Church, and each of us individually as we are being sanctified, bearing fruit in every good work.

While ghosts are mentioned in the Scriptures in Matthew 14:26, Mark 6:49, Luke 24:37 and 24:39, the Greek word that is translated as "a ghost" in the text is **phantasma**, which simply means "an apparition or spirit." This word does not imply the spirit of a deceased person, but rather a non-human entity that is immaterial. Ghosts are demonic apparitions that appear in our reality. Whereas, demons are immaterial spirits that deceive, lie, stand against God, and seek to torment, influence, and possess personal and geographical territory in our created order.

We know from Scripture that there is a hierarchy within the demonic order and their assignments are as diverse as the holy angels that are obedient to God. Ghosts and paranormal activity are an off-limit activity for Christians, with the only exception being deliverance from them and dominion over them by our authority in Christ.

There is one last thing to consider before we move on: In 1 Samuel 28, Saul sought out the medium at Endor in an attempt to contact Samuel the dead prophet of God. This is a unique circumstance and the only example in Scripture of someone contacting the dead. In the narrative, Saul is desperate, alone, and demonically tormented. The Holy Spirit has departed from him, his kingdom was being given to David, and he was facing an immense threat from the Philistine army. With heaven being brass to all of Saul's attempts at knowing his future, he crosses the spiritual line and seeks illegal spiritual information. There is not a more terrible and tormented position for a person to be in than the position in which King Saul finds himself.

Scholars and theologians have addressed this passage with two views.

The first view is that a satanic spirit appeared to Saul, feared him, and sealed his doom at the hands of the Philistine army resulting in his death. The second view is that Samuel did indeed appear to Saul through the sovereign choice of God, giving the reader a descriptive illustration of the depravity, judgment, and rejection of Saul by God which warns us to always stay obedient, repentant, and trust in the Lord.

Regardless of the position we hold about this narrative, the truth remains that this interaction was unique and not normalized or endorsed as something Christians should seek to do or be involved in. Just because it happened once, never makes it the norm, especially in terms of the spiritual gifts God gives to His children that are spiritually legal and encouraged by the Scriptures for us to use as ministry to others. We do not need to chase extra-Biblical experiences in paranormal expressions to experience spiritual

power or revelation because the Holy
Spirit lives within us.

CHAPTER 4

The Return of Christ

"Behold! I tell you a mystery. We shall not all sleep,
but we shall all be changed…"
1 Corinthians 15:51

One of the most hopeful doctrines
of the Christian faith is eschatology, or
"the study of the end times, when Jesus
Christ returns to receive His Bride, the
Church, and inaugurate the eternal
order; i.e. life that will always be."
Christians in every age of Church history
have placed their vision towards the

future and found comfort knowing that amid the injustice, chaos, wars, famines, and natural disasters, that there will be a day - the Lord's Day - when Jesus will come and make all things right redeeming and renewing the whole created order at His coming.

Biblical justice reveals itself when God takes that which is not right, true, or just and makes it right, true, and just. This happens in the first fruits way through the agency of the Church and then in its fullness at the return of Jesus Christ. The Nicene Creed of AD 325 says, "He suffered and the third day rose again, ascended into heaven; From thence He shall come to judge the quick and the dead." This one doctrine is the doctrine that fuels our passion for Christ, gives us hope in the waiting, and has inspired almost 2000 years of gospel preaching and demonstrations of our faith that have reaped a global harvest of sons and daughters for the Father.

Christians throughout history have divided themselves into various camps regarding The Doctrine of Last Things. These camps are the Partial-Preterists and Premillennialists. However, the one thing all Christians have in common regarding the return of Jesus Christ, is that He does *indeed* return, judges the living and the dead, then restores creation to its Edenic design.

Eschatology is my favorite discipline of study because this doctrine touches every aspect of the Christian life here as we wait for our departure, either of this body in death or by the glorious return of our Lord Jesus Christ. What we believe about God and believe about the End Times directly influences our level of hope, courage, boldness, and quality of life during the times we live. If we believe in an apocalyptic end, then we may live apocalyptically focused lives. If we believe that we are part of a renewed, hopeful, and glorious people of God who are co-laboring with Him to usher in the return of Christ, then we will live hopeful vision focused lives. No matter what our view is, we can all heartily agree to the truth that Jesus is returning to make all things new and recolor our wonderful cosmos that has been marred by corruption resulting from the Fall.

In the previous chapters, we have learned that both the righteous and the unrighteous dead are conscious after death in an intermediate state of existence in either Hades or heaven while waiting for the return of Jesus, His judgment, and then eternal life in a sinless and incorruptible renewed creation in the very presence of the Godhead on earth. Though the book of Revelation provides an amazing amount of detail regarding the cosmic spiritual battle of the Kingdom exerting dominion over the devil and his minions, it is written in the symbolic and hyper-bolic language of type and shadows, cultural idioms, and mysteries that cause our minds to consider the glorious triumph of Jesus. It is important to realize we have very few literal interpretive opportunities to know decisively *how* exactly the return of Jesus Christ occurs. However, the good news is that 1 Corinthians 15 gives Christians an amazing amount of detail of how the return of Christ takes place in human history. Let us walk through the text and be encouraged in the hope of a resurrected body, the return of Jesus Christ, and the death of death itself.

1 Corinthians 15 - The Roadmap of the Return of Jesus

In 1 Corinthians 15, the Apostle Paul answers the Corinthians' questions about the resurrection of Jesus, the resurrection of the body, the return of Christ, and the eternal order. This chapter gives a simple outline that is easy to follow and provides a lot of detail regarding what Christians believe about the end of the New Covenant Age. It is one of the most hopeful and victorious sections of Scripture in our New Testament. It is Scriptures like these that cause our minds to consider the overarching victory of the gospel and of Jesus Himself over the Babylonian system in which we live, especially as we consider the times we are living in that are broadcasting defeat to the Church and the loss of individual rights here in the United States where I live.

I am writing this book towards the supposed end of the COVID19 pandemic, and if one only looks at the firehose of negative news stories, fearful predictions of the prophets of doom, the disintegration of the social fabric, and the growing political divide in the United States, it would be easy to lose hope and consider that the Church is defeated and that we have no hope. Fortunately, Scripture provides a different narrative of how Jesus Christ and His Bride, the Church will overcome the evil one and have dominion at the return of our Messiah.

In history, empires rise and fall. It may be the end of America's

Judeo-Christian Era, but it is certainly not the end of the kingdom of God, or the end of the mission of the Church in the world to demonstrate the glory and power of God as we save, heal, and deliver those in the grip of the devil. It is just another Babylonian system waiting to be evangelized out of existence like Ancient Rome. The destiny of nations is determined by the activity or inactivity of the people of God who live in those nations.

1 Corinthians 15:1-4 opens with a reminder of the gospel that Paul had preached to them. Paul begins by reminding them that our story of redemption, renewal, and eternal life begins with a death. In verse 3, Paul says that Christ died for sins according to the Scriptures, that Jesus was buried and then rose again on the third day. It is at the center of the Christian faith that Jesus died for sins. There is no other sacrifice or atonement that saves humanity from the wages of sin, which is death and the judgment of

hell. Any attempt at minimizing the sacrificial atonement of Christ is to the peril of those who embrace theologies that deny Jesus died as a result of the individual and collective sin of humanity. Our entrance to life will always be begins with the simplicity of the gospel, that Jesus died for sin, rose again, is ascended, and is coming again to judge the living and the dead. The gospel of Jesus Christ is the epic story of death and resurrection, cosmic spiritual warfare, forgiveness, restoration, miracles, signs, wonders, and eternal life all summed up in a new creation. It is an amazing experience to love God, love the Son, and commune with the Holy Spirit. This is all made possible by God moving providentially throughout human history towards His loving and benevolent end.

In the next movement found in 1 Corinthians 15:5-19, Paul gives bold examples to the Corinthians of the people who personally witnessed the living and resurrected Jesus Christ.

In the text, Paul mentions Peter and the Twelve and then goes on to tell them about an occasion when Jesus showed Himself alive to more than five hundred people. Paul says that most of them were still alive to testify about the encounter. It is almost as if Paul is encouraging the Corinthians to check out the story and discover for themselves the veracity of the resurrection of Jesus. Paul explains that Jesus appeared to His half-brother James, then to other apostles, and finally to himself.

The reason that Paul provides all of these examples is so that the resurrection of Jesus Christ is the hinge point and the central doctrine of Christianity. Our faith is founded on this fact. It proves the Father has accepted the sacrifice for sin and that Jesus conquered death. Therefore, Jesus is the only Man, the Second Adam, who can impart eternal life to those who trust Him. The Corinthians were questioning if there was ever a resurrection of

Jesus or even a general resurrection of the dead. Paul said that without the resurrection of Jesus Christ, your faith is futile "and you are still in your sins." Christianity implodes and falls apart if Christ was not raised from the dead. This is why Paul gives such strong evidence of the resurrection.

1 Corinthians 15:20-26 then goes on to provide the specifics and the progressions of the return of Jesus Christ. The first progression in the return of Jesus Christ is that Jesus is the first fruits of a resurrection to come. Jesus is the guarantee for every Christian to believe and have the sure hope that we will be resurrected in an incorruptible resurrection body. In the text, Paul describes the righteous dead as "those who have fallen asleep." These words are a comforting and grace-filled way to describe the body as it waits for the resurrection. The text says that if all humanity dies by Adam, then those who believe will live by one Man, Jesus Christ, the Second Adam. In 1 Corinthians

15:23, Paul begins to define each step of the progression to the renewal of all things. Let's look at the text and see what he says:

> "But each in his own order: Christ the firstfruits, then at his coming those who belong to Christ. Then comes the end, when he delivers the kingdom to God the Father after destroying every rule and every authority and power. For he must reign until he has put all his enemies under his feet. The last enemy to be destroyed is death."

The eschatological progression of the return of Jesus is laid out for us in an easy-to-understand manner. First, Jesus is the example of the resurrection for all people who believe. Second, when Jesus returns He brings with him everyone who has believed are with Him in heaven. Third, the end comes and Jesus destroys every enemy that stands against His rule and reign. The word "destroying" in the Geek is the verb **katargeō**, which means "to render idle, unemployed, inactivate, inoperative, to cease, annul, and abolish." This implies that Jesus Himself actively pursues everything that stands against His authority and ends its opposition. The fourth movement demonstrates that Jesus delivers the kingdom to the Father when Jesus has won every victory.

Lastly, verse 25 implies that Jesus is currently ruling and reigning and is actively and progressively subjecting everything that stands against Him in this age, through the Church and then in totality at His second coming. Then the last enemy of Christ to be defeated is the destruction of death. These few verses contain the compressed narrative of how Christ returns and puts all things under His feet. The eschatological machinations are gloriously simple. Jesus, through His Church, is conquering opposition spiritually, and in the future,

He returns with the righteous dead, wins the victory, and then consummates the end of all things. 1 Corinthians 15:50-54 describes the return of Jesus in stunning detail that indicates the instantaneous transformation of the living and the righteous dead and at the same time, the eternal order is unveiled. This whole section of Scripture should encourage us like the Corinthian Church to walk the walk of faith, endure, and persevere over the evil one in all things as we live our lives in Christ.

The Resurrection Body

Again, 1 Corinthians 15 gives intimate details about the resurrection body that we will receive when the renewal of the created order comes at Jesus' return. Paul uses various examples in nature from seeds that are buried and then transform into a new life that is wholly different from what was planted. This is a wonderful metaphor for the resurrection body that is waiting for us who believe. The text goes on to differentiate between the types of flesh and bodies that are found in the created order as an example of the type of body that we will receive when we are resurrected.

The resurrection body is different from our fallen flesh which is subject to aging, injury, disease, and death. Our earthly body is sown in corruption; our resurrection body is raised incorruptible. Paul says that "our resurrection body is in the likeness of Jesus' resurrection body." It will be immortal, incorruptible, and capable of transcending the laws of physics as we know them in this fallen cosmos that is waiting for renewal.

It is amazing to consider that we will never again be in pain, age, sustain injury, or be subject to death, or any type of discomfort. Just like Jesus, we will enjoy all the goodness that the renewed creation gives. After Jesus' resurrection, He ate, enjoyed the company of His disciples, walked through walls, and appeared out of nowhere. Scripture is not exactly clear what our existence on the renewed earth will be like but we can assume it will be amazing to live a life that is free from the chains of the Edenic fall. We can therefore look forward to a perfect body, a perfect mind with perfect emotions, and freedom to explore the creation as we worship and serve the Godhead on a renewed earth.

The beautiful doctrine of the resurrection of the righteous dead gives meaning and hope in the life we live today. Death is not the end of us but opens to us the unfolding of life that will always be. This transcends the pain and suffering of the human experience and adds value to every life that has ever lived.

The Death of Death

As 1 Corinthians 15 wraps up Paul's Holy Spirit-inspired revelation, he quotes Isaiah 25:8, "When the perishable puts on the imperishable, and the mortal puts on immortality, then shall come to pass the saying that is written: "Death is swallowed up in victory." "O death, where is your victory? O death, where is your sting?" The parallel passage being Revelation 20:14, where Death and Hades are thrown into the lake of fire gives us a picture that death dies, and in the absence of death, there is the only life that emanates from God.

Death is a constant reminder of the injustice that the serpent perpetrated in Eden against the Sons of Adam and the Daughters of Eve. The whole human race was orphaned from a Father and died in Eden. Death may have a temporal victory now because our mortal bodies die, but in a future where Christ renews the cosmos, death itself will die.

Sex and Marriage and the Resurrection Body

Jesus was asked by the Sadducees in Luke 20:27-40 about the resurrection with a question that revolved around the Law of the Kinsman Redeemer. When a married brother died without producing an heir, the other brother or brothers who were alive were obligated to marry the widow and produce an heir for the deceased brother so that the wife would be cared for and the land inheritance would not cease from the brother's bloodline. The Sadducees gave Jesus the example of a woman who was married to seven brothers consecutively without producing an heir and then she dies. They ask Jesus, "In the resurrection, therefore, whose wife will the woman be? For the seven had her as wife." Jesus' answer to them teaches us that in our resurrection bodies we will be equal to angels, we would not marry, and we would be true sons (speaking of position, not sex/gender) of the resurrection, saying we "cannot die" meaning we would be immortal and live forever.

Since Christian marriage is the spiritual metaphor and prophetic picture for the covenant concept of being joined to Christ (two becoming one), the prophetic picture of marriage would be fulfilled in the resurrection.

Marriage is God's design for repro-duction and for the enjoyment of sex. Therefore, having no marriage means no more need for sexual intimacy. If we believe the orthodox view that sexual expression and intimacy in marriage is between a man and woman through a theological and typological lens, what emerges is that sexual intimacy is a firstfruits taste of heaven. The sexual ideal and design of God in marriage is trust, tenderness, closeness, joy, exploration, and climax that has the potential to create a life that God ordained.

Sex and marriage are prophetic metaphors for the fullness that is prom-ised to us in the resurrection as we are reunited with God without shame and in perfect union. Ephesians 5:22-33 is a beautiful illustration of this truth. More Christians should read the text through this lens, and heal their marriage as they become a prophetic picture of the union of Christ and His Church to come.

In the resurrection, we will still be able to know each other since we maintain our distinct identity and form in the resurrected body. However, in terms of marriage, family, and sexual intimacy, it is a gift that we enjoy in this age and the agency by which God receives generations of people to enjoy and love. Christians in the Modern Era need to do a better job in advocating for sex-positivity in marriage, the joy of raising children, and the power of a healthy family as a witness for Christ. Everyone on earth comes from a family and a healthy godly family is almost as powerful for Christ as directly preaching the gospel because it speaks to everyone. Every married couple desires a good marriage and a good family. As Christians excel in family, we will draw many to the Church of Jesus Christ.

In the next chapter, we will explore what the new heaven and the new earth will be like and what we might be doing in the new heaven and earth. Though the Bible does not give us the specifics of exactly what our resurrected body life will be like, we do gain enough information to encourage us to antici-pate that it will be amazing. The imagery in the Scriptures that describe the new heavens and new earth invites our imaginations to wonder at the mystery of life that will always be and empower us to color outside the lines of the restraints of our current created order. Can we fly, can we deep dive under-water, can we travel the cosmos and visit other heavenly bodies? Who knows? In a renewed creation, all these things may be permissible by God.

CHAPTER 5

The New Creation

"And he who was seated on the throne said, "Behold,
I am making all things new." Also, he said,
"Write this down, for these words are
trustworthy and true."
Revelation 21:5

Eternity is written on our hearts and the created order is longing for the freedom that comes with a new cosmos. The Apostle Paul wrote, "for the creation waits with eager longing for the revealing of the sons of God." In some way the creation itself is aware that it is subject to the wages of our sin and what manifests is the life and death cycle in our world. We see such evidence all around us when we observe creation. The animals live and die, our beloved pets wear out and pass away, trees lose their leaves, the vegetation grows for a season and then it is harvested, and finally composted to nourish the next cycle. Even the food that sustains human life undergoes a death and resurrection cycle. We harvest, we eat to be strengthened, we eliminate waste, and we age. Even a slight awareness of these things reminds us that creation itself is subjected to the effects of the Fall. In the futility of a life cycle that creation cannot escape, God promises a renewal in the revelation of Messiah at His coming.

In Revelation 21, we have amazing symbolism and allegory in the text that opens our minds to consider the infinite dimensions of the new heavens and new earth that God has promised those who believe. Revelation 21:1 paraphrases Isaiah 65:17-19, which reads:

> "For behold, I create new heavens and a new earth, and the former things shall not be remembered or come into mind. But be glad and rejoice forever in that which I create; for behold, I create Jerusalem to be a joy, and her people to be a gladness. I will rejoice in Jerusalem and be glad in my people; no more shall be heard in it the sound of weeping and the cry of distress."

Notice the new heaven and the new earth are not speaking of the heaven where the Godhead dwells but rather a fresh, newly created order that is free from the influence of the Fall and full of the presence of the God-head. God is personally intertwined with the new creation and there is no opportunity for pain, error, sin, or corruption because the new heavens and the new earth perfectly reflect His illumination. Light is the allegory and symbol for the illuminating effect of God on the minds, hearts, and resurrected bodies of people and the revelation of perfection in the new creation cosmos. The whole world is changed into a wonderful place where we can explore the endless beauty of God and His new creation in a new resurrection body.

The Revelation 21 paraphrase of Isaiah 65:17-19 brings a more personal revelation of God because He is actively comforting His people and consoling their hearts. In Revelation 21:3-4, it says that God Himself will be with His people in some revealed and tangible way that we can only dream or speculate about in this age. In Revelation 21:4, God personally wipes tears and declares that death will be no more. Because the wages of sin is death, the absence of death implies a sin-free cosmos for His children to enjoy. Later in the text, John quotes the Lord; "Behold I am making all things new" and then later, "It is done." This implies that the new creation life was released in the atonement of Jesus Christ in first fruit grace as people are born again, walk with Him, advance the rule and reign of Jesus Christ, and recolor society with His value systems.

The work of the atonement was to be accomplished and finished, and now humanity is witnessing and waiting for the unfolding and revealing of the new creation in the return of Jesus Christ. When we consider this, we can see that the gospel is more than simply the declaration of eternal life in Christ by faith, it is the announcement of the promise of Eden restored and the first experience of eternal life lived on the inside of those who believe in Jesus. That new creation life, the born again experience is lived on the inside of us, is the witness and the motivation to share this new life with the world around us and to conform ourselves and the world around us to the image of Christ.

The promise of entrance into the new heaven and earth is found in the promise of the endurance and perseverance of our faith in this age. Revelation 21:7 tells us those who conquer will have the inheritance of the new heaven and new earth as sons and daughters. The glorious truth in the text is contrasted to those who have chosen to reject Christ and not endure in faith until the end, which is their judgment and death at His coming.

We should not read works into the text, rather, we should be acutely aware that our life in Christ is a type of marriage covenant with Jesus which demands every Christian to be a faithful Bride and love God as much as possible in the context of our situations and to partner with our call to be conformed to the image of the Son. Those who are excluded from the new heavens and new earth are described in the text as the cowardly, the faithless, the detestable (de-stable), murderers, sexually immoral, those that practice witchcraft, idolaters, and the people who traffic and believe lies. The text says that their portion, part, or destiny will be the lake of fire which is the "second death" that we learned about earlier in this book. This chapter in Revelation is a major hindrance for the advocates of the universalist view of hell because there are people who are cast into the lake of fire.

As Revelation 21 progresses, John continues to speak to one of the seven bowl judgment angels and is taken by the angel to a high mountain where John sees the New Jerusalem descending from heaven where God dwells. It is described in unimaginable beauty and the details in the text are full of symbolism of twelves, names, and stones that all communicate facets of truth in the symbology regarding the beauty, and the overarching authority and dominion of the God-head. The imagery contained in the text is an invitation for the reader to explore each symbol and discover not only theological truth but find personal encouragement to live in deep faith as well. Revelation is one of the most underestimated Scriptures for developing spiritual formation, worship, and prayer in the lives of believers. Most Western Christians place it solely in the context of eschatology and miss its power to inspire our confidence in God that leads us to worship praise, and obey Him in our daily lives.

At the end of Revelation 21, no Temple is present in the New Jerusalem because God is its Temple. Like Abraham, we gain God as our very great and precious reward for a lifetime of serving and loving Him.

The New Heavens

In 2 Peter Chapter 3, we receive more information about the Day of the Lord which is the return of Jesus

Christ. This is a day that will come as a surprise to the people on earth and a day where the whole created order will be transformed by a fire that brings about the dissolution of the cursed creation and the revelation of new heaven and earth that will reflect God's perfection in the original design. The text indicates that even the heavenly bodies, the stars, and planets, will be transformed into a sinless reality.

It is interesting to meditate on what the sinless heaven would be like. Most people do not view space as a sinful reality. However, when we consider that space reveals our mortality in ways that no other environment does. We can see that where death is present the curse from the Fall prevails. Space is an environment of chaos in an ever-expanding vacuum. It is also a beautiful demonstration of God's creative power and it is an example of chaos theory in living color with black holes, collisions of heavenly bodies, and the death of stars, in an ever-expanding reality of paradoxical disorder and order. Since death and chaos are possible in space, new heavens have been promised that are somehow remade into a benevolent reality where life and order prevail and the curse is removed. Will humans be able to explore a perfect universe? The Scriptures do not give that answer to us conclusively, but what we can say is that where there is no death, there is only life.

God's first act of creation was creating the heavens or the cosmos as the foundation from which earth would be contained and placed in perfect proximity within the cosmos to sustain life. It reveals to us that as God created the cosmos, life-sustaining planet earth was in the mind of God. In many ways Revelation 21 could be called the re-creation account because the perfection that was manifested in the first creation before the Fall, would be made new at the coming of Jesus Christ. The multi-faceted layers of renewal in the cosmos all began with Messiah and His death on a cross and His resurrection.

If death, chaos, and corruption all came from Adam, then another Adam, the Messiah Jesus Christ, is the inaugural hope of the new heavens and new earth that was promised to humanity through the Scriptures. This fascinating marriage of theology and quantum physics is a new frontier just waiting to be explored by Christian philosophers, theologians, and physicists. Just as Romans 1 teaches us that the creation itself is a witness of God's invisible attributes and His eternal power, the study of the cosmos through the discipline of physics may be the strongest apologetic for creationism that will emerge in the future. Christianity may experience renewal as quantum physics reveals God's invisible attributes.

In the ancient world, we learned that the heavens were thought to be constructed with God dwelling in the highest heavens, and then the second and first heavens would be where Satan and his dominion of unholy angels operated. The great spiritual battles between Michael the archangel and the Prince of Persia in Daniel 10 took place in the first and second heavens. The new heavens will be the end of the second heaven satanic and demonic influence. The spiritual war has already been decisively won through the atonement of Christ, but the fullness will be manifested in the new heavens and new earth. It must be a terrifying coming reality for Satan and his demons knowing that their demise and destruction is impending doom. Revelation 12:12 says that "the devil has come to the earth in great wrath knowing his time is short." Indeed, the time is short for Satan considering the length of this temporal age compared to the infinite reality of a new heaven and new earth that do not wear out or cease to be.

Though Satan and his demonic hordes inflict pain and propagate sin, their opportunity for evil will be over in an instant, when Messiah, Jesus Christ is revealed and the new heavens are birthed in a fire that gives new creation life. We can look forward to new heavens full of the perfect benevolence of God's goodness and new heavens that are free from the spiritual warfare that is waged against humanity by Satan and his demons.

The New Earth

Although the Scriptures do not answer every question we would have about the new earth, we can conclude from 2 Peter 3 and Revelation 21, the new earth will be perfect and free from death, disease, toxins, and anything else that is opposed to eternal life and perfection that reflects God's nature and character. Like the cosmos, the new earth will be born by a fire that inaugurates a reality where humanity lives free from the construct of time and the power of death. Revelation 21 gives us an interesting detail in its first verse, where the text says that "there will be no sea." From a cursory reading of Revelation 21:1, we would conclude that there are no oceans in the new earth. However, later in Revelation 22, we see a river of life that feeds and heals the new creation. So we know in some way, water is present in the new earth. It is important that we do not read too much into a text, or discount the implications of the imagery contained in the text.

The subject of a new heaven and new earth are difficult concepts and God in His wisdom painted the pictures with very wide brushes to invite us into such mystery. God gave us enough information to know that there is a new heaven and earth on the horizon in the time-space continuum, and enough knowledge to know that it is enveloped in a sinless perfection that is a return to His original design of a perfect created order.

As we consider the wider meaning

in the text about the absence of a sea, we are invited to take a deeper dive into the ways that the sea or seas have been used in Scripture for us to discover an expanded concept for the reader. In ancient thought, the sea or seas were a fitting metaphor for the masses of humanity and the chaos and unpredictability of the whole aggregate of people groups on the earth.

The Greek philosopher Homer often used the created order to build similes and metaphors to communicate his philosophical concepts. Terms like mountains, seas, stars, heavenly bodies, hills, lightning, hail, and thunder are all common metaphors in Scripture that speak to realities about God or His nature and character. It was common in the ancient and Classical ages to use nature to communicate a layered message to the reader or hearer that communicates complex ideas and thoughts through those metaphors.

In Scripture, the metaphor of

the sea or seas is commonly used to describe people groups that are in rebellion against God, Gentile nations, and the common disorder in the masses of humanity on the earth. Psalm 65:7 uses the metaphor of roaring seas to describe the roar and confusion of the Gentile nations who are in rebellion against God. Ezekiel 32:2 also uses the metaphor of seas to describe the power of Pharaoh and Egypt and prophesies a lamentation concerning God's judgment on Egypt for oppressing the nations surrounding them. However, the most moving metaphor in Scripture that describes people groups and nations is found in Revelation 13, which describes a beast rising out of the sea. Both the symbolism of beast and sea in this text describes the ascent of the Roman Empire as the oppressor of the civilized world who was being animated by Satan's desires and rose to preeminence over the people groups in the ancient world.

Now that we can see that the

sea or seas can be used as a metaphor for nations and people groups, it is most likely that the new earth that is described in Revelation 21:1 saying "and the sea was no more," describes the divine order of the nations of the world being in harmony and alignment with God as they follow His heart. It is the end of the chaotic rule of tyrants, dictators, socialists, communists, and politically corrupt governments that rob wealth and oppress the people of the world. Satan's operating system of the perversion of the people is chaos, democide, confusion, division, racism, slavery, and oppression of people groups for exploitation and the propagation of pain.

Lastly, the Greek word for "sea" used in Revelation 21:1 is a word used to denote the Mediterranean Sea. The Romans referred to the Mediterranean Sea as **Mare Nostrum** (our sea) and the ancient world considered the Mediterranean Sea the maritime highway that ensured Roman hegemony over the classical civilized world. Revelation 21:1 may describe a world in which the Roman Empire is an archetype for governments that are under satanic leadership that has ceased to be. The conclusion being that under the rule and reign of the Godhead, the nations of the earth are free from sinful societies, cultures, governments, and tyrannical leaders because their leaders are no more. It is an earth that knows no war, no famine, and no political intrigue. The new earth is a safe place for the nations to enjoy God's manifest presence and enjoy the amazing prosperity that will freely flow from the Godhead.

The new earth is the fullness of the vision God cast when He gave humanity the mandate to rule, reign, and manage the creation He gave them before the Fall. Genesis 1:26-28 describes the perfected dominion mandate over the earth that the Lord charged Adam and Eve to express as they co-labored with God. They were mandated to be fruitful and multiply, rule and subjugate the earth, and enjoy its bounty. Though people do not reproduce in heaven or the new earth, the redeemed will still fulfill some part of the dominion mandate as humanity lives out God's desires for the planet in their resurrection bodies.

Perfect Order

The last thing to consider as we close this chapter on the new heavens and the new earth is that perfect order is established. The prophets Isaiah, Ezekiel, and Daniel give us snapshots of a perfectly ordered planet earth in their writings. There are two passages in Isaiah that are the most prominent in describing what that perfect order is like: Isaiah 11 and Isaiah 65. Both these passages teach us that predators and prey will be in harmony and children would be able to lead them and not be harmed. Isaiah 65 describes a reality where the lion - the apex predator - will eat grass, and snakes will no longer hunt, kill, and eat prey. We should not take these passages literally, rather, we should see how they demonstrate that in the perfect order there will be no more predatory killing. There is also an expectation to a return of the sinless innocence of the created order that is free from evil and death.

The new heavens and new earth are a perfected and ordered cosmos that contains no disorder, no death, and mirrors the perfected design of God's mind and heart for His creation. The existence of error points our attention to the fact that we are living under the constraints of a fallen world colored by the effects of sin.

A perfect order is devoid of chaos. We could look at any ecosystem or universe in the new heavens and new earth and see a perfect alignment, order, and design in motion. We would find no atrophy or aging. Instead, we would find the complexities of the created order functioning at optimum and synergistic harmony in an immortal and eternal cosmos. Scripture does not give us the intimate details about the age to come, but it does give some building blocks of knowledge that give us some indication that this perfect order reflects a perfect God, who promises to redeem humanity and give us a new creation to enjoy because the serpent and his seed have been annihilated. What a wonderful future to look forward to! A future free from accident, error, and corruption.

In the next chapter, we will look at how this life, despite its seasons of pain and imperfections, is still enjoyed, and how living with the hope of new creation life gives us encouragement to live in joy and hopeful expectation. Living with a new creation vision puts the issues of life in a perspective that destroys the fatalism and depression that the enemy wants to sow into people's lives.

CHAPTER 6

CELEBRATING LIFE

*"Behold, what I have seen to be good and fitting is to
eat and drink and find enjoyment in all the toil with
which one toils under the sun the few days of his life
that God has given him, for this is his lot."*
Ecclesiastes 5:19

In previous chapters, we have
explored the theological thoughts
and constructs about eternal life, the
resurrection body, the return of Jesus
Christ, the judgment of the sinner, and
the renewal of all things. Since we have
drawn so much attention to the hope
of things to come, the effects of sin, and

the corruption in the world as a result of the Fall, it would be appropriate to spend some time encouraging us in this life too. This life is a gift from God, and God desires us to experience His goodness, love, grace, loving-kindness, forgiveness, and provision in the here and now.

The created order may be imperfect and marred by the Fall, but God designed the human experience to be as joyful as possible as we wait for our departure or His return. I ask you, dear reader, to take time to see all the ways that God has blessed humanity in this life. As we reflect, we can think of beautiful memories with family and friends, as well as those life experiences that are cathartic and defining, and we can see God's goodness throughout the creation that we enjoy daily.

As Christians, we believe the Holy Trinity is omnipotent, omnipresent, and omniscient. Believing these core truths about the Godhead places us in a world where God is in the midst. The Reformation Fathers used the Latin phrase, **Coram Deo**, to describe this reality. It is living with the awareness that all life lives before the face of God. It implies that all Christians live before God, under the authority of God, and live their lives to glorify God in all things. Living with this vision for life is the pathway for us to enjoy this life that God gave to us because we see God involved in every dimension of our lives both personally and corporately. This is the foundation for a Biblical worldview.

Most Western Christians have been deeply influenced by the Platonic worldview and live in a dualism that divides the cosmos between the immaterial from the physical. The Greek philosopher Plato constructed the cosmos in terms of form (which is perfect immortal immaterialism) and matter (which is the physical reality that Plato defined as base and subject to corruption). Plato saw the world constructed in a dualism of the perfect immaterial realm versus an imperfect physical realm with the hope of death releasing the body from the immortal soul. It is important to acknowledge the influence of the Platonic worldview on Western Christian theology because this worldview has influenced the way Christian theologians have approached the subjects of hell, the immortality of the soul, heaven, and most importantly the sovereignty of God. The colored lenses of Platonism have been the filter by which most Classical Western theologians have described the Person of God and His relationship to His creation.

While not all aspects of Platonism are wrong, Western Theologians today should begin to rethink these very wide and deep subjects through the lens of a better scholarship that seeks to reform and harmonize Western theology by adopting a Biblical worldview and construct of the cosmos that is based on Hebrew or Eastern philosophy and thought. Fortunately, today many Western theologians are taking advantage of the volume of Eastern and Jewish scholarship that is available through the internet in the areas of sociology, archeology, and cultural studies. There has never been a time in Western Christian theology where the East/West divide has been erased by technology while informing and empowering Western theologians to reform Western Christianity to an expression that is more Apostolic and closer to its origins in the East.

The major difficulty with the Platonic worldview is that it influences Christians to accept thoughts that prevent them from seeing God's intimate involvement in the world and the lives of His people. Platonism produces a theology of God where we perceive Him from being separated from His creation. An Eastern/Hebrew worldview promotes a cosmology where God and His creation interact in relational ways that are authentic with both parties moving each other's hearts.

The Integrated Biblical Worldview

One way that encourages Christians to celebrate life and enjoy the wonderful world which God created for humanity is to see the world through an integrated cosmology that mirrors the narratives we see in Scripture. From the beginning of the creation narrative, it is through the lives of Moses, Abraham, Moses, and David we see God moving in relational ways, encountering these men in the context of a real relationship, where each party moves the heart of the other.

In addition to this, we see the supernatural realm completely connected and immeshed into the whole cosmos, not in a pantheistic way, but rather in a way where the omnipresence, omniscience, and omnipotence of God are intimately involved in the creation. We should think that God is filling creation. In this cosmology, the physical realm is not separated from the spiritual realm but both the natural order and spiritual order are integrated and interdependent. In the Scriptural integrated worldview, the natural realm follows the spiritual realm. In this worldview, prayer becomes relational, God's actions in the world are relational, and the influence of evil and sin is in the context of spiritual warfare and the free will choices of people.

To see the world through Biblical eyes is a pathway for realizing that there is no divide between the secular and the sacred. Certainly, there are sacred spaces for worship and hosting God's presence either in our pursuit of God or in corporate gatherings that are set apart to reverence, praise, and adore God. However, our life in Christ and His leadership in our lives touches every part of our humanity as Christians.

Having an integrated Biblical worldview teaches us that our work, our family, our marriages, our finances, and our leisure time are all parts of the human experience before God. God enjoys us as we live our lives. As a Father to children, the Lord guides, celebrates, and intervenes on our behalf in amazing ways that take place in the context of a relational covenant through Christ.

The integrated worldview frees Christians to enjoy a whole new and living reality that plays out every day. Having this understanding empowers us to care about the nations in which we live, love our neighbors, and co-labor with God to redeem society and culture. The Great Commission in Matthew 28:18-20 mandates nothing less than the salvation of whole aggregates of people. The integrated Biblical worldview agrees with this expectation from Christ for the Church universal, to be successful in our mission.

When we look at societies' cultures, sociologists have identified seven spheres of a cultural organization that emerge when aggregates of people come together. These seven spheres of expression in culture are:

- Religion
- Family
- Government
- Economy
- Education
- Media
- Arts/Entertainment

As God is omnipresent, omniscient, and omnipotent, He is in all cultures, especially the ones that recognize His presence and authority. Good leaders of nations recognize their accountability to God and seek to lead a people closer to Him. A moral people realize God's authority and live in the awareness of His authority. As a result of this awareness, safe societies emerge where crime is low, the nuclear family is secure, and economies prosper.

Now that we have a simple definition and understanding of the two world views, the Platonic worldview and the integrated Biblical worldview, we can see that aligning with the integrated worldview helps Christians live with a hopeful expectation of experiencing God's goodness in every area of our lives.

Enjoying the Blessings

One of the most amazing sections of Scripture that highlights the intimate involvement of God in our everyday lives is Deuteronomy 28:1-14. What emerges from studying this section of verses, is the revelation that God is involved and cares about His people. He desires to bless His people in all things. This section of verses begins with an invitation to obey God.

Since we know that no one is perfect before God and that none of us can keep the Law in totality, we must rely on the atonement of Jesus Christ for the forgiveness and remission of our sin. The sacrifice of Jesus Christ on the cross and His resurrection is the guarantee that the Father accepted the sacrifice of Christ and His blood atones our sin.

Earlier in this book, we learned that the atonement of Christ affected the whole created order. Through the atonement of Christ, the cosmos will be made new. Jesus, being the perfect Man (Adam), was the Torah incarnate during His ministry on earth. Jesus demonstrated what it looked like to live in perfect obedience to the Father.

Since Christ was a perfect Man, He was a perfect sacrifice for the sins of humanity. Jesus Christ imputes to us what we are not. He alone makes us holy. He sanctifies us and justifies us before the Father by our faith in Him. Therefore, we have access to the Deuteronomy 28 blessings. Jesus, who knew no sin, became sin for us, removing the curse of the Law thus granting us access to grace, blessing, and divine favor. This is great news!

It is good news, that now our obedience to God is predicated on our relational experience with Christ. We can now grow in obedience to

Christ by the Holy Spirit extending grace for us to live in ways that we could not before. The promises in Deuteronomy 28:1-14 are available to us based upon our faith in the atonement of Christ and our willingness to conform to His image through the power of the Holy Spirit. The command to obey God in Deuteronomy 28:1 is fulfilled in Christ and now we can grow in that obedience through our relational covenant with the Holy Trinity as New Covenant believers.

Deuteronomy 28:2 promises the people of God will emerge as the preeminent people in the world. The Church of Jesus is the people of God in the world today representing Him, praying for His will and kingdom to come, asking God for provision, serving Him, loving others, and healing the hurts of others. Our unique role as salt, light, and leaven in the world speaks to the missional nature of the Church as we co-labor with God to redeem and reform the world around us.

The Church of Jesus Christ is successful because God is successful. As Christians submit to God's leadership and co-labor in the world with Him, we will overcome the evil one and the world that is under his shadow. Christians have access to the thoughts of God, the emotions of God, and the wisdom of God because we have His Word and the Holy Spirit in us. The Deuteronomy 28:2 promise of being set high above the nations of the earth is possible because of the delegated authority of Jesus that is imparted to the Church, both individually and corporately. Our expectation should be for success for the people of God. When we are successful, the whole world around us gains grace for the goodness of God to be manifested in society.

Deuteronomy 28:1-14 continues with blessings would overtake the people of God. What a beautiful word picture in the Hebrew text of the people of God being overcome and taken hold of by God's blessing of divine favor in our lives! The text says every-where we go we would be blessed. This kind of blessing is a comprehensive and holistic blessing that extends to our children, our agriculture, our economy, and even the deliverance of our nations from our enemies who seek to destroy us.

Deuteronomy 28:1-14 goes on to state that the fear of God would be made manifest in the people around us because they can see the glory and power of God's covenant is with us. The text says that we will abound with prosperity and that God would open His very own treasury and pour out rain on the land and blessing on the works of our hands. What a wonderful expectation to believe and experi-ence God's divine favor in our lives!

The expectation of Deuteronomy 28:1-14 is that our whole life experi-ence on the earth is marked with the goodness of God manifesting in every area of our lives. Notice the text still acknowledges the existence of hardship and the possibility of pain. However, during pain and hardship, God in providential love and grace will work through all things to bring about His best for us. Romans 8:28 says, "And we know that for those who love God all things work together for good, for those who are called according to his purpose."

Every Christian should have the expectation of the blessing of God in our daily lives within the context of our lives. Christians live in all kinds of circumstances and socioeconomic categories. However, the expectation is that within our respective places in society, we experience the work of God's hand to bring about His best. We should be hopeful and happy people who have great confidence in God's ability to provide. Jesus, in the Sermon on the Mount, exhorted us to surrender to God's Fatherly care and live in His goodness. We should enjoy the blessing of the human experience as we sojourn in this life with God, family, and friends. We should enjoy the journey towards heaven and the return of Jesus Christ.

Conclusion

H opefully, this book has answered your questions about immortality, eternal life, heaven, the resurrection, and hell, or at least inspired you to seek the Lord concerning these subjects. Like any book about complex theological themes, it is almost impossible to exhaustively answer every question or concern one might have. But *Life That Will Always Be* is a good starting place to begin the journey of living your life here with a purpose, vision, and a hopeful expectation of God's goodness in this life and in the eternal one to come. In all things, we should praise God who has lovingly Fathered the human family throughout all generations since the beginning of time. This world may be subject to the pain, death, and imperfection resulting from the Fall, but God in His great grace has worked through the time-space continuum to bring about the promise of Messiah and is still working with us until the revelation of Jesus Christ when He returns.

In 2 Corinthians 1:3, the Apostle Paul declares that God is the God of all comfort to those who believe. As we have experienced this comfort from God we can extend it to others so we can comfort them in their trials and pain. The whole drama and epic of the narratives in the Scriptures revolve around the promise of an Eden that was lost to sin, and its promised restoration that will come from the Man who would redeem humanity from sin, defeat the serpent, and restore us to Eden. Scripture is a glorious saga that inspires and invites us to experience the very Person of God inside us. Through Scripture, we are offered the wisdom of God and His promises of eternal life so that we may live in the fullness that this current life has to offer. I pray you will experience God's goodness here and live with the awareness that one day you will step into the life that will always be through your faith in Jesus Christ. ***CARPE DIEM!***

ARISE: Spiritual Formation for the Apostolic Reformation

This book will give you theological on-ramps to personal spiritual growth and renewal. Designed to draw you closer God, *ARISE* will help you understand His nature and character, while activating you into partnering with Him in your daily lives. A useful tool for study groups, *ARISE* has provoking questions at the end of each chapter to help you evaluate your spiritual life.

IN VIA: Spiritual Meditations for the Lent Season

This 40-Day devotional book was written to empower Christians to connect with Jesus, grow spiritually, and release renewal in their lives. This book is a dynamic tool to help grow you into deeper faith and develop your spiritual senses as you journey through the Lent Season. Endorsed by Jake Hamilton, one of the leaders of the modern worship and prayer movement:

"Rob Covell is a catalytic teacher who consistently leads us back to the Word and gives us a sense of its vitality in our every day experience. This devotional will give readers an opportunity to interact with the heart of God as Rob leads us through the beauty and majesty of the Lent Season. You will be inspired and transformed as you journey through these 40-Days."